THE NEW NORMAL

THE NEW NORMAL
The Transgender Agenda

LISA NOLLAND
CARLOS D. FLORES
BRITTANY KLEIN
JAMES LOPEZ
ROBERT OSCAR LOPEZ
DANIEL MOODY
CARYS MOSELEY
JOHN NOLLAND
PETER SAUNDERS
RICK THOMAS
JULIA GASPER

Wilberforce Publications
London

First published in Great Britain in 2018 by
Wilberforce Publications Limited
70 Wimpole Street, London W1G 8AX
Wilberforce Publications Limited is a wholly owned subsidiary
of Christian Concern

ISBN 978-0-9956832-5-9

Printed in Great Britain by Imprint Digital, Exeter
and worldwide by CreateSpace

Contents

PREFACE
DR LISA S. NOLLAND

'The New Normal' Conference was first of its kind. Held in London in November 2016, it was a rich interdisciplinary feast for academics, professionals, parents and those who were seriously worried about the 'Cultural Marxist' revolution and its successful 'long march through the institutions' (Rudi Dutschke).

'Missing In Action'
Solid church organisations and leaders have largely been 'Missing in Action' and that for various reasons. Some have slept through the revolution while others stay busy with good but non-controversial matters which fail to counter the claims of the revolution. Some insist that 'preaching the gospel' will sort things, unaware that the gospel's very essence and terminology (such as what sin even is!) is being hollowed out and re-defined. Others frame these matters in terms of theology, focusing on the individual and their behaviour, while ignoring the wider context: they don't 'do politics'. Because what we are up against is a 2018 version of 'That Hideous Strength', such a view is woefully inadequate. The revolution is fast becoming the 'New Normal' for all sectors of life.

Resistance
However, a few pioneers have been willing to forge new and positive paths of resistance. This book represents some of their best thought. Happily, it includes not only careful theoretical analysis and evaluation but encourages – indeed demands – active engagement and response. In fact, one of the main reasons we are where we are at the moment is

because good, decent people who should have known better decided to sit this one out — for them, perhaps, it was just not worth it! But our children's welfare, present and future, is at stake. There is too much to lose.

The Transgender Tsunami

Since the conference, one of the most significant developments has been the tsunami of transgender rights, which arguably pose an even greater threat than the imposition of lesbian, gay and bisexual rights across society.

In transgenderism, hard physical realities of bodies dissolve, and the only thing that matters is one's subjective reality ('I identify as Jane today'), which the rest of us have to collude with by using the right pronouns and so forth.

And it does not stop with pronouns but proceeds to showers and sleeping quarters for, say, 'progressive' Girl Guides (26 November 2017). It is not 'best practice' even to inform parents if their daughters are sharing toilets with biological boys who claim they are girls.[1]

Is this really okay? Do we want our daughters showering with lads who insist they are girls? Would we as adults want to shower with adults of the opposite sex? And children are much more vulnerable.

Practical Pushback

Schools can be a key area for engagement. At the moment, the Christian Legal Centre is walking with a brave couple, Nigel and Sally Rowe, who are protesting the imposition of this flat-earth (but politically correct and powerful) ideology – transgenderism – in their children's school on the Isle of Wight. Standing with them and their legal representation is one great resistance strategy. Bringing a representative from Christian Concern/Christian Legal Centre to your church would raise awareness in an important way.

Other important pushbacks include promoting Parent Power (www.parentpower.family: 'Know your rights and how to make a difference') and ex-gay ministry (https://www.core-issues.org/: 'Challenging gender confusion; upholding science and conscience'). Mass Resistance UK (http://www.massresistance.org/index.html) is another excellent resource for responding to the revolutionary madness.

Waking up the Church

As well, it is high time that those who see and are appalled by this madness to hold to account church and parachurch organisations which claim a 'this world' involvement.

These organisations receive significant amounts of money, have extensive resources and prestige and yet are unwilling to be where the battle is the hottest. In fact, frequently they do not even acknowledge there is a battle! If the leadership cannot hear concerns, perhaps they can hear the loss of funding.

Money talks! Are you supporting organisations which are willing to engage or ones which, sadly, are part of the problem through their complicity and silence? Denial is understandable but, at the end of the day, unacceptable, especially for leaders.

As Bonhoeffer reminds us, 'Silence in the face of evil is itself evil: God will not hold us guiltless. Not to speak is to speak. Not to act is to act.'

Finally, prayer is vital. This is a supernatural fight of epic proportions and we are doomed unless we first engage there. Groups to pray regularly into and about these matters are essential. Pray 2018 Churchills and Bonhoeffers onto platforms and into positions of influence! Leadership is woefully lacking here (among other things). Could we start to get serious and engage in prayer?

The Consequences Are Too Great

I end with a quotation of Ayn Rand, which I think apt: 'We can ignore reality but we cannot ignore the consequences of ignoring reality'. The New Normal will ultimately fail, and that on its own terms. Truth will out, sooner or later – it has to. But in the meantime the casualties will continue to mount. Will you join us to save our children, indeed our church and country, from this disastrous movement?

Lisa Severine Nolland

[1] http://www.telegraph.co.uk/news/2017/11/26/guides-allows-boys-identify-female-shower-girls/

THE TRANSGENDER AGENDA

WHAT IS THE THEOLOGICAL APPROACH THAT THE WESTERN CHURCHES SHOULD TAKE REGARDING TRANSGENDER ISSUES IN RELATION TO CHILDREN?

DR CARYS MOSELEY

What is the goal and purpose of a constructive theology addressing how transgender issues affect children today?
– to glorify God
– to provide a framework for the education and care of children which will ensure their mental and physical health and wellbeing
– to bring up children who will grow up to be resilient in the face of the transgender attack on reality
– to live faithfully as God created humans male and female for the sake of having children. Children have a need and therefore a right to be reared by their parents in such a way that they can grow up to be at peace with being male or female as their created nature requires.

God loves each one of us as his creatures, and Christians are meant to show God's love in respecting the created nature and uniqueness of each person.

The New Testament calls upon Christians to '...be transformed by the renewing of your mind...' (see Romans 12:2). This includes Christ's understanding of the Old Testament and creation.[1] As Christ the Son pre-existed the historical Jesus, as the second person of the Trinity, he was present at the creation of the first man and woman (John 1:1-3; Ephesians 3:9; Colossians 1:15-20).[2] Christian theologians have always understood 'Let us make man in our image' to be the speech of the Trinity.[3]

We need to look at the history of theology, particularly the Patristic era and the modern period, because the Church has faced many of these problems before, and Christian theology already has adequate means of dealing with them.

Basic Christian anthropology
How three related Christian doctrines, formulated on the basis of the Bible by the Latin and Greek Fathers, including theologians of a Jewish background, provide the necessary foundations for this teaching about children

The three doctrines are: (1) the creation of humans in the image and likeness of God; (2) the creation of humans as male and female in order to have children; (3) the doctrine of the special creation of the soul at conception. Why focus on these three doctrines? First, because they constitute the foundation of Christian anthropology. Secondly, since apologetics for Christian doctrine enables us to make sense of empirical research. Repeatedly in Genesis, God says about the creation, including human beings, that it is 'very good'. It is 'very good' that God created human beings, and that he created them male and female for the purpose of marriage and having children. It is very good that each person is a unique creature from conception onwards, a person to be cared for by his or her parents. It is the soul and not only the body that constitutes the uniqueness of the person.

Image and likeness of God as comprising the soul and the body

Two patristic themes are of interest here. First, the understanding that the image of God refers to both the spiritual and the physical aspect of human creatureliness. Second, the Church Fathers debated whether the Bible revealed that God intended human beings to procreate sexually even if sin had never entered the world. Irenaeus of Lyons (d. 177), following the tripartite anthropology found in the New Testament, claimed that man as spirit, soul and body was made in the likeness of God. He refused to define human beings according to one of these alone, formulating doctrine in relation to the teaching of Paul in 1 Thessalonians that Christians should strive to preserve themselves until the return of Christ:

> For by the hands of the Father, that is, by the Son and the Holy Spirit, man, and not [merely] a part of man, was made in the likeness of God. Now the soul and the spirit are certainly a part of the man, but certainly not the man; for the perfect man consists in the commingling and the union of the soul receiving the spirit of the Father, and the admixture of that fleshly nature which was moulded after the image of God.... And for this cause does the apostle [Paul] explaining himself, make it clear that the saved man is a complete man as well as a spiritual man; saying thus in the first Epistle to the Thessalonians, 'Now the God of peace sanctify you perfect (perfectos); and may your spirit, and soul, and body be preserved whole without complaint to the coming of the Lord Jesus Christ.' Now what was his object in praying that these three – that is, soul, body and spirit – might be preserved to the coming of the Lord, unless he was aware of the [future] reintegration and union of the three, and [that they should be heirs of] one and the same salvation?[4]

Justin Martyr (d. 180) defended the value of the body in the eyes of God against those who would devalue it. His argument was that the flesh is valuable because God formed it and because the creation of the rest of the world is also of value to God.[5] The fourth-century bishop Epiphanius of Salamis, who came from a Jewish background, also defended the notion of the body partaking of the notion of the image and likeness of God.[6] Whilst it might seem that these theologians were stretching the definition of being made in the image and likeness of God, given that most theologians held God to be incorporeal and immaterial, it is evident that they were motivated by the belief, held by all Christians, in the resurrection at the end of history whereby believers would be given a new re-created body. This hope coupled with fidelity to God motivated care of the body as opposed to contempt for it. It is the reason that ritual damaging of the body is forbidden in the New Testament (Colossians 2:23).

Sexual reproduction – intended to be pre- or post-lapsarian?

God created human beings as male and female so that they would reproduce sexually even had there been no Fall into sin. This is made clear by the fact that the statement on creation of male and female and the command to 'be fruitful and multiply' is found within the account of the seven days of creation in Genesis 1. The reason this matters is that historically some theologies question whether sexual reproduction only emerged after the Fall, perhaps as some sort of divine punishment for sin. Such theologies have tended to interpret the Genesis narratives as implying that individual human beings were originally both male and female.[7]

The special creation of each soul by God at conception

Special creation is probably the doctrine most familiar to non-Christians thanks to debates about when life begins and whether abortion is permissible. Whilst special creation can be inferred to be true of how God created Adam and Eve in the Genesis narrative, given that they had no ancestors, does it necessarily follow that it is true of all people since the Fall? The question was posed by Augustine of Hippo, due to the difficulty of balancing original sin with special creation of souls.[8] The uniqueness and therefore special creation of each human body was not in doubt, being visibly verifiable (no two human bodies, even comparing parents and children, are exactly alike). The question Augustine asked was whether each human soul is created specially by God at conception or whether soul generates soul. Augustine left the question open, but subsequent theologians argued in favour of special creation of the soul. One of the principles at stake here was and is the equal value of soul and body.

The Church Fathers also rejected Origen of Alexandria's flirtation with the idea of the preexistence of souls before birth and even before creation.[9] This is important because the notion that the soul exists before conception and even the creation of the world lends itself to the idea of a gendered soul. The idea that a person was 'born in the wrong body' has long been the standard first-person narrative presented by self-identified transgender persons in public debate in order to justify being allowed to undergo medical and social gender reassignment (previously known as 'sex-change' treatment).[10] Assuming that this declaration of belief is sincere (and there are many grounds for doubting it) the question arises as to what might be believed to be the cause of 'being born in the wrong body' (i.e. in the body of the sex opposite to which the person claims they truly belong).[11] The cause cannot be the parents; no parents can do anything to bring about that their unborn child is to be a member of one particular sex. There has to be a deeper, cosmic cause attributed by the transgender person to the predicament of being 'born in the wrong body': God, gods, or nature. In cultures like our own where Christianity is the main historical religion and influence upon people's belief (even including agnostic and atheistic rejection of belief in God), to state 'I was born in the wrong body' is effectively to imply that God caused or allowed to happen that a particular person (whether or not this be understood to be a soul or mind) who was before birth of a particular gender was inserted into the sex opposite that gender. So in plain terms, a 'male' soul or mind or person was inserted into a female body, or a 'female' soul or mind or person was inserted into a male body. There is no indication whatsoever in the Bible, which has always been taken to be divine revelation by Christians, that God has ever intended to do such a thing. In addition, to make such a claim, with the logical presuppositions that it necessitates, goes against the doctrine of special creation of the soul at conception. Whilst the doctrine of the preexistence of the soul does not necessarily entail a further doctrine that the soul is gendered, it does allow for it.

Nowhere in the Bible is it stated that souls (or spirits) are male or female. None of the Church Fathers taught this either. In Genesis it is clear that the purpose of God in creating humans as male and female is sexual reproduction – something that, being immaterial, mere souls (or spirits) by themselves cannot do. This basic Christian metaphysical assumption is what enabled feminism to grow in officially Christian countries in the Western world. As such, nobody should be surprised that the present Christian critique of the ideology of gender, the notion that the soul or spirit (or mind, a concept which has been used far more in the modern period) can be 'male' or 'female' apart from the body, shares some basic assumptions with the tradition of secular feminist critique of transsexualism and transgenderism, from Janice Raymond through to today.[12] It is this that the transgender movement is challenging, and why it has promoted the idea of 'brain sex'.[13] It was the idea that a person's sense of 'gender' is rooted in the brain that was advanced as the justification for permitting sex-change surgery on the NHS at the taxpayers expense by Alex Carlile when he was Liberal Democrat MP for Montgomeryshire.[14] At the same time it can be argued that the notion of 'brain sex' is a materialist version of a *belief* which in previous ages would have been referring to the mind or the soul. This is because younger people in the West are less likely to believe in the existence of a soul or a mind as immaterial entities metaphysically distinct from the body. The same people tend not to believe in God either. (Indeed it is worth asking ourselves whether the concept of gender, seeing as it is considered an aspect of mind, has not replaced the soul as a belief in sectors of the population. See the surveys towards the end of this chapter.)

The likely origins of gender dysphoria

The truth is that there exists a body of clinical literature as well as anecdotal testimony regarding the roots of gender dysphoria (previously known as Gender Identity Disorder) that spans decades of psychiatry and psychology.[15] In this context it may seem subjective and arbitrary to counter the claim to be 'born in the wrong body' with Christian doctrine about creation. The question remains as to how such an insistent feeling came about, of belonging to the opposite sex/gender even though objectively speaking a boy or man cannot have any real experience of being a girl or woman, or vice versa. The very fact that Christian doctrine insists that the unique human person begins life at conception is important here as it places a moral requirement upon us to take the unborn child seriously as a person with needs from conception onwards. We now know (even if many in Western society don't want to admit it too much) that the unborn child is profoundly sensitive to how his or her parents treat him or her.[16] Unborn children do sense in the womb if they are loved and welcomed by their parents or not – and that includes sensing whether their mother and father really would prefer a child of the opposite sex. In the same way, children who have been born also can tell this. Treating a child as a member of the opposite sex, usually because one or both parents are disappointed the child was not of that sex, is known to confuse children and likely to be a factor in the development gender dysphoria in them.[17] It really isn't that difficult to understand, especially given widespread acceptance of the fact that children readily internalise parents' and other people's attitudes and feelings towards them regarding a whole host of other issues.

Notice how Genesis tells us that Adam and Eve before the Fall were 'naked and unashamed'. They were clothed only after the Fall. It is not an accident that Paul's statement 'For I am not ashamed of the gospel' echoes Genesis. Cross-dressing is deemed a sin in Deuteronomy 22:5 and also 1 Corinthians 11. This should really serve as a serious warning to ask ourselves why it is deemed so; what could be the problems that such a prohibition is intended to prevent? The obvious answer is the confusion stemming from the fact that wearing the clothes of the opposite sex both signifies an existing mental confusion and reluctance to identify with one's own sex, and also can reinforce this. (Being secular in nature, most clinical literature on children and adolescents with gender identity problems does not discuss this.) One unusual case has been recorded of a small boy developing gender dysphoria in response to his mother's depression after she had an abortion of a baby girl who had Down's Syndrome.[18] In light of this it is worth asking to what extent a general pro-choice ethic, which carries with it both a lack of respect for the individual person created as soul and body, along with a diminished willingness to handle abortion-related grief and trauma, might have contributed to the magical ideas involved in gender dysphoria. It should be said that there are also cases where a person who developed gender dysphoria did so due to being abused in this manner by other family members or by peers.[19] Gender dysphoria can be one reaction to being sexually abused, developing a fantasy that life as a member of the opposite sex would be less painful and more rewarding. Finally, nobody should discount the influence of mass media, including television programmes which normalise 'trans kids', websites targeted at impressionable young people (e.g., hypnosis programs telling young men they can be 'women'), and internet pornography involving transsexualism.[20]

'Gnostic' theologies ancient and modern

The century or so of psychiatric, psychological, and sociological writing on transgenderism mostly does not discuss the topic in relation to comparison of religious beliefs. Here I provide a theological explanation for what the French philosopher of psychiatry Pierre-Henri Castel calls 'la déraison' (unreason) in a person's wish to 'change sex'.[21] Reference was made above to the claim to be 'born in the wrong body' as a belief or dogmatic claim. It is equally appropriate to consider it as a claim to secret knowledge which goes against our knowledge of the person involved. In the ancient classical world where Christianity was born, several pagan religions made various claims to knowledge or 'gnosis' (the Greek word for knowledge) about the divine, the spiritual realm, human beings, and the world. 'Gnosticism' is a category invented by modern academics to categorise many of these ancient religions. Some groups sometimes tried to borrow Christian concepts or often claimed to be the true form of Christianity secretly passed on by the apostles, or even Jesus, by word of mouth.[22] Thus, these so-called 'gnostic' religions competed with the New

Testament witness by invoking an alternative oral tradition of teaching which purportedly went behind the text of the New Testament. The sorts of claims made and behaviours found in the transgender subculture bear some comparison with some of these gnostic pagan religions.

The most obvious echo of transgenderism in classical antiquity, certainly with regard to bodily mutilation of sexual characteristics, is the cult of Cybele, the Great Mother Goddess, from Asia Minor.[23] The priestesses were women and the cult supposedly involved the castration of young men. The cult of Cybele became part of the official cult of Rome from 204 BC. The Naassene sect which existed in the early centuries AD probably developed from the cult of Attis, and practised castration and cross-dressing.[24] Hippolytus of Rome criticises them.[25] That the cult of Cybele became incorporated into the Roman imperial cult is perhaps significant because Christians were persecuted for refusing to worship and sacrifice to the Roman imperial cult. According to the Roman historian Tacitus, Nero was the first emperor to persecute Christians in 64 AD.[26] This he did to scapegoat Christians for the Great Fire of Rome which he himself was rumoured to have started. Although Christians were an unpopular and despised minority anyway, it is worth asking why Nero hated them so much. According to Nero's biographer Suetonius, he had entered into a mock marriage with a young male slave named Sporus whom he dressed as a woman.[27] Tacitus, Suetonius, and the historian Dio Cassius also relate that Nero had previously undergone a public 'marriage' ceremony to a freedman, this time with Nero himself taking the role of the 'bride'.[28] Thus we can see a certain transgender identification by Nero. Thus, when considering the problem of cross-sex/gender identification, it is important to comprehend that the early Christians were dealing with rival religious groups and some elements of Roman culture which were deeply hostile to their anthropological vision. Many of the religious groups which the early Church Fathers criticised as attempting to masquerade as 'true' Christianity differed fundamentally from the Church in terms of the doctrine of creation, anthropology, and sexual ethics.

What happened to these movements? The early Church leaders disciplined them and threw them out. However, this in itself would not have caused these groups to die out, for as long as pagan religion was permitted in the Roman Empire they would have existed. There is a more likely reason internal to these religions as to why they declined and disappeared. Their sexual ethics, if acted upon, would not have been conducive to their demographic growth – quite the opposite in fact. Any movement which condemned marriage as evil, or which practised cross-dressing and castration, or which produced no teaching about childrearing, would not have attracted men and women who wanted to marry and bring up their children in that movement's teachings. It would only have been able to increase through recruitment, not also through childbearing.

There was a body of texts which can be argued to have been a vehicle for negative attitudes to the Christian doctrine of the creation of humans as male and female during most of European history. Those are the Hermetic texts, written in Greek but originating in Graeco-Roman Egypt and translated into Latin in the Middle Ages.[29] They told the creation myth of the Primordial Androgyne or Hermaphrodite (see below) who later 'fell' and split into male and female. What this meant was that human sexual difference was not considered a good part of creation, as in Genesis, but as a consequence of a fall into sin. The Hermetic texts were known to Christian theologians and sometimes quoted by them. At times in the history of Christianity there has been the temptation for some to read Genesis through the lens of the Hermetic texts, and to speculate that human beings were originally an 'Adam' who was a Hermaphrodite (encompassing both male and female elements) or an Androgyne (neither one sex or the other). These texts were central to the tradition of alchemical writings in the medieval and early modern period, mostly from Germany and Britain, and to the Western esoteric tradition more broadly.[30] (It is relevant that early psychiatric literature, most of it in German and English, on transsexuals from the first half of the twentieth century moved between these two poles when discussing the psychology of patients.) Two of the most influential theologians in the Western esoteric tradition in the modern period espoused the belief that the soul is gendered – Emmanuel Swedenborg and G. W. F. Hegel, both heterodox Lutherans. Swedenborg believed that male and female souls could be married out of the body and in heaven.[31] Swedenborg's theology, an esoteric form of Christianity, developed during the 18th century, became very influential in the USA upon movements like the Transcendentalists, New Thought, and so on. This may explain why the transgender ideology has become so prominent among liberal or progressive religious groups in the USA.

In all of this cross-sex/gender identification, it is important to realise that what is being implied is an abnormally sharp dualism of soul or mind and body, one that mentally healthy people do not experience. As hinted already, there are several different problems that can be included under the label 'gender dysphoria' (or whichever label is currently acceptable). Castel tells us that the first use of language akin to 'woman trapped in a man's body' was used by Karl Heinrich Ulrichs in the late nineteenth century.[32] Perhaps it is relevant that Castel notes Ulrichs specifically spoke of a 'woman trapped in' not 'born in' a male body.[33] This suggests a less dogmatic and more metaphorical approach, arguably one slightly less insistent upon physical treatment. It is relevant that the clinical literature on gender dysphoria does show that sufferers may also have certain mental health problems. These may include schizophrenia, Obsessive-Compulsive Disorder, Body Dysmorphic Disorder, anorexia, among other things. The case of Daniel Paul Schreber, the author of the most famous memoirs in history written by a madman, touches upon this. Daniel Paul Schreber was a German judge who suffered a nervous breakdown and a series of delusional psychotic episodes in the late nineteenth century. In his extraordinarily lengthy book *Memoirs of My Nervous Illness* he claimed to have received divine revelation as well as a female genital organ and to have become pregnant.[34] Psychiatrists and psychoanalysts like Sigmund Freud read his *Memoirs* with fascination. Debate still goes on about it today. Historian of psychiatry Louis Sass believes that Schreber's case was symptomatic of a tendency in modern Western culture and philosophy, comparing his case to what the French philosopher René Descartes had to say about himself, and what the German philosopher Ludwig Wittgenstein wrote about the nature of reasoning as a philosopher. Sass picked up on what others have also noticed in Descartes' works, which is that he displayed symptoms of psychological abnormality in seeing the mind as superior to the body and the body as some sort of object or machine, and other people likewise.[35] It is worth considering some possible parallels between this sharp mind-body dualism and the sharp dualism of 'gender' and body – both claimed and normalised by the transgender movement. Seen in this light, it should be obvious that it should not be encouraged, rather that steps should be taken to prevent and mitigate it.

Finally, it is of obvious interest that Daniel Paul Schreber set out his own theology. Schreber believed the human soul to be contained in the nerves of the body. God, according to him, was 'only nerve, not body, and therefore akin to the human soul'. Schreber professed agnosticism about creation, whether God had created all things or only the organic world. Following Kant and the Deists, he denied that God intervened in human affairs during our lifetime. He believed in the transmigration of souls. He said that his voices told him that people were allotted lower status in the next life, perhaps as a punishment. He believed in gradual improvement of the soul towards the state of Blessedness, and that the male state of Blessedness was superior to the female state. For him, the ultimate destiny of all souls was to merge with other souls and remain aware only of being part of God. Thus, personal identity was very weak. Schreber claimed that his voices started to speak to him of two gods, Ahriman and Ormuzd, the two gods of ancient Persian religion. The Persians or, more recently, the Germans, not the Jews, were God's chosen people. From all this we see clearly that Schreber's beliefs were anti-Christian. What is distinctive about Schreber is that his delusions ended after a while; he was not claiming to have been 'born in the wrong body' nor was he concealing a fetish. However, the same substance pertains to all of these, namely the untruth that someone somehow at some point really 'is' a member of the opposite sex to their actual sex, and that this is somehow some greater truth which everybody else ought to accept, celebrate, and normalise.

Eunuchs are not a 'third gender' in the Bible
Currently there is a movement arguing for legal and social recognition of a 'third gender' or genders other than male and female.[36] This movement is slowly making progress in Western countries and elsewhere. With regard to understanding and applying the Bible, some people

have argued that eunuchs are a sort of 'third gender'.[37] The problem with this argument is that 'gender' is not a concept found in the Bible and is not a concept originating from within Christian theology or philosophy at all.[38] The contemporary movement for a 'third gender' wants people who identify themselves as 'non-binary' to be addressed by specific 'third gender pronouns' ('ze' instead of 'he' or 'she').[39] By contrast, eunuchs in the Bible are always referred to as males, so are understood to be men (or by extension women) who were sexually mutilated (Isaiah 56, Jeremiah, Matthew 19, Mark 10, Acts 8).

Why secular critics have not succeeded in stemming the tide of transgender ideology

Over time, many people from different professions and all walks of life have criticised the increasing tendency for the medical and legal professions to give in to the demands of people who want to live as members of the opposite sex. Increasingly, however, one senses a pattern of underlying censorship and self-censorship. The question that needs asking is why reasonable, secular criticism has not succeeded. Here it helps to study the little evidence there is regarding public opinion on this matter.

In 2014, ComRes found that something like 75% of British people would prefer it if the NHS did not fund sex-change (gender reassignment) surgery.[40] This was in a very secularised society. Clearly, most people see it as a private 'lifestyle choice' and not at all a medical 'need'. In 2015, Sky News found that a significant proportion of British people morally disapprove of gender reassignment. Only 25% thought the NHS should pay for gender reassignment.[41] This matches the ComRes finding. This rose to no more than 30% among adults aged 18-34 year old. In 2015, a Huffington Post survey showed parents are torn between not wanting their child to have a sex change yet going along with it anyway.[42] Only 11% of parents said they would strongly resist. This undoubtedly correlates with the similar percentage of British adults who attend religious worship weekly. The 25% of parents who said they would be 'happy' if their child wanted a sex-change correlates remarkably with the 25% in the previous two surveys who think the NHS should fund sex-change/gender reassignment. In 2016, Survation polled British people on attitudes to gender for the Fawcett Society.[43] Opinion on gender identity in Britain is split. More than half (56%) think there are two genders – male and female – and less than half (44%) think gender can be a range of identities. Women take a more fluid view than men – 48% of women think gender can be a range of identities compared to 39% of men. Older people hold more prescriptive views on gender – 65% of over 65s think gender is binary compared to 44% of 18-24 year olds, with both views significantly differing from the 56% national average.

For men and women in equal measure, belief that there are two genders declines down the age range in a similar pattern to decline in traditional Christian sexual ethics and belief in God. This is to be expected, but also shows that some people work with the idea that gender is just another word for sex, whereas others realise that it has several meanings that are completely subjective. A very large percentage of younger adults believe that there are more than two genders. Only 41% of women aged 18-24 believe that there are only two genders.

Belief that there are several 'genders' probably correlates with the rise of atheism and the collapse of belief in the Christian God. It also probably correlates with the decline in belief in the soul. The Survation survey for the Fawcett Society very clearly shows that gender is a matter of belief, or at least an opinion, as it asks people which of two statements best describes their 'view'. It is also clear from this survey, as from generally surveying the history of the concept and its spread, that it is a very recent belief that has changed and that can change very quickly. It is very unstable.

The psychotherapist Az Hakeem used to run the only psychotherapy group for people who regret sex-change surgery in Britain, in the Portman Clinic in London. In an essay published in 2007 he clearly expresses scepticism about surgery as a treatment for gender dysphoria, a scepticism based on the profound sorrow expressed by clients in this group.[44] However, some transgender activists attacked him for writing this essay and he more or less recanted his views after transgender activists forced the Royal College of Psychiatrists to cancel a conference entitled 'Transgender: Time For Change' in 2011, where he was scheduled to speak. He now works entirely in the private sector. The truth is that it is not unknown for dedicated professionals to be attacked by some of the very people their work aims to help. Yet my question as to why secular criticisms have not been heeded by those with the power to do so remains. Given this widespread rejection of the belief that gender reassignment should be allowed on the NHS, even among younger people, why have the secular critics of the transgender ideology not succeeded? I believe that despite herself being an atheist, the late French psychotherapist Colette Chiland provides the answer:

The death of God (by which I mean the collapse of the omnipotence of tradition, of the source of the law in an absolute Beyond that cannot be called into question), the beneficent affirmation of human rights, and the dubious development of individualism – all these allow the individual to claim the right to change sex without recognizing any prohibition that might stand in their way.

At the same time as the individual feels himself to be a subject of law, there is a corresponding weakening of his consciousness of being also a subject of duty, and of his feeling of responsibility towards other people in general and his family and friends in particular. Respect for private life takes precedence over any other consideration, and is deemed (by the European Court of Human Rights) to include the right to change sex.[45]

Chiland sees transsexualism as transgression, the violation of a law or prohibition. She refers to the Deputy Public Prosecutor of France, Fabre, invoking the finger of God as Creator in Genesis 1 as an absolute prohibition on 'sex-change'. She then remarks that 'many transsexuals declare that they believe in God', saying that God caused them to be born into the 'wrong body'. In essence they are blaming God for their problems. In colluding with this claim, whether it be sincere or not, the powers that be are also colluding with blaming God. Christians have a spiritual and moral duty to take the opposite path to that one in all the work that they do, be it preaching, teaching, pastoral care or advocacy.

Notes

[1] On Christ's understanding of the OT see John Wenham, *Christ and the Bible*, London: Tyndale House, 1972.

[2] The pre-existence of Christ at creation was affirmed by the Church Fathers, cf. Irenaeus of Lyons, *Against Heresies* 1.22.1, 2.2.5, 5.18.3.

[3] On Genesis 1:26-28 as Trinitarian speech, as well as for an overview of Patristic commentary on these verses, see Andrew Louth (ed.), *Genesis 1-11, Ancient Christian Commentary on Scripture, Old Testament I*, Downers Grove, ILL: Inter-Varsity Press, 2001: 27-37.

[4] The translation used is that from:
http://www.earlychristianwritings.com/text/irenaeus-book5.html

[5] The translation of Robertson-Donaldson is quoted from: http://www.earlychristianwritings.com/text/justinmartyr-resurrection.html

[6] Epiphanius of Salamis, *Panarion* 70.3.

[7] These will be discussed further below. For general differences between

the Latin Fathers (especially Augustine) and the Greek Fathers on the question of sexual reproduction, see Andrew Louth (ed.), *Genesis 1-11*: 37-41.

[8] For a good general discussion of the complexity of Augustine's reasoning on the soul's origin, see Gerald O'Daly, *Augustine's Philosophy of Mind*, London: Duckworth, 1987. An introduction to patristic theologies of the soul before the fourth century can be found in J. N. D. Kelly, *Early Christian Doctrines* (5th edition), London: A & C Black, 1977: 174-83.

[9] See Kelly, *Early Christian Doctrines*, 344f., on Gregory of Nyssa's critique of Origen.

[10] A good overview of the issues (under the term 'transsexualism', more recently eclipsed by the term 'transgender') can be found in Colette Chiland, *Transsexualism: Illusion and Reality*, English translation, London: Continuum, 2003. Chiland was unwilling to recommend psychotherapy clients for surgical treatment. It is increasingly rare to find publications by such mental health professionals, no doubt due to the normalisation of pro-transgender perspectives in mental health.

[11] Grounds for doubting the sincerity of this narrative in some individual cases involving adult males include the evidence that many males presenting themselves for gender reassignment to the medical profession are in fact in the grip of a fetish called autogynephilia, whereby they fantasise about being women. This is distinct from discerning whether gender dysphoria is the core problem of the individual, or whether their discomfort with living as a member of their sex is not related to another problem.

[12] The classic study is Janice Raymond, *The Transsexual Empire*, Boston, MA: Beacon Press, 1979; London: The Women's Press, 1980.

[13] Some of the basic problems with the theory are discussed in: https://sexnotgender.com/brain-sex-does-not-exist/

[14] http://hansard.millbanksystems.com/commons/1996/feb/02/gender-identity-registration-and-civil#S6CV0270P0_19960202_HOC_108

[15] The bibliography by Pierre-Henri Castel covers the period 1910-1998: http://pierrehenri.castel.free.fr.

[16] See the evidence marshalled in Thomas Verny with John Kelly, *The Secret Life of the Unborn Child*, London: Warner Books, 1993.

[17] Zucker and Bradley discuss specific cases from their own clinical experience, whilst criticising the research in the field for being incomplete. Kenneth J. Zucker and Susan J. Bradley, *Gender Identity Disorder and Psychosexual Problems in Children and Adolescents*, New York: The Guildford Press, 1995: 212-215. It is important here to recognise that parents who have gone to Gender Identity Clinics worried about their children's cross-sex/gender identification appear to be either confused themselves or sincere in their desire for their children's welfare. However, it needs to be admitted that some parents simply wish to have their child's

tendency to identify more with the opposite sex/gender to be confirmed. These are the parents that ought to be under suspicion for having concealed from the therapist the fact that they treated their children as members of the opposite sex/gender, always having wished for a child of the opposite sex/gender, and secretly cross-dressing them, or at the very least for having neglected their children and left them with other persons, perhaps not entirely aware of their influence upon them. Obviously no therapist has written of specific cases of unproven suspicions of this kind as it would be inappropriate.

[18] Susan Coates and Richard C. Friedman, 'The etiology of boyhood gender identity disorder: A model to integrating temperament, development, and psychodynamics', *Psychoanalytic Dialogues: The International Journal of Relational Perspectives* 1(1991) 4:481-523; the case is discussed by reference to trauma in Susan W. Coates and Mary Sue Moore, 'The complexity of early trauma: representation and transformation', in Domenico Di Ceglie with David Freedman (eds.), *A Stranger in My Own Body: Atypical Gender Identity Development and Mental Health*, London: Karnac Books, 1998.

[19] A wide-ranging discussion can be found in Domenico Di Ceglie with David Freedman (eds.), *A Stranger in My Own Body*. Examples given by Christians involved in this area include the following: Denise Shick, *My Daddy's Secret*; Denise Shick and Help 4 Families, *When Hope Seems Lost*, Xulon Press, 2011; Gae Hall, *He can never be She*, USA, 2013; Walt Heyer, *Gender, Lies and Suicide*, 2013.

[20] Colette Chiland refers to 'mediagenesis' in Colette Chiland, *Transsexualism: Illusion and Reality*, (English translation), London: Continuum, 2003: 19-20.

[21] Pierre-Henri Castel, *La metamorphose impensable: Essai sur le transsexualisme et l'identite personnelle*, Paris: Gallimard, 2003.

[22] On gnostic reintrepretations of Genesis and the teaching of Jesus, see Gerard P. Luttikhuizen, *Gnostic Revisions of Genesis Stories and Early Jesus Traditions*, Leiden: Brill, 2006.

[23] Jaime Alvar, *Romanising Oriental Gods: Myth, Salvation and Ethics in the Cults of Cybele, Isis and Mithras*. Translated and edited by Richard Gordon, Leiden: Brill, 2008.

[24] Maria Grazia Lancellotti, *The Naassenes: a gnostic identity among Judaism, Christianity, classical and ancient Near Eastern traditions*, Münster: Ugarit-Verlag, 2000.

[25] Hippolytus of Rome, *The Refutation of All Heresies*, 5. http://www.earlychristianwritings.com/text/hippolytus5.html

[26] Tacitus, *Annals* XV.44. http://penelope.uchicag.edu/Thayer/e/roman/texts/tacitus/annals/15b*.html

[27] Suetonius, *The Life of Nero*, 28. http://sourcebooks.fordham.edu/halsall/ancient/suet-nero-rolfe.asp

[28] Tacitus, *Annals* XV. 27. Suetonius, *The Life of Nero*, 29. Cassius Dio, *Roman History* 27. http://penelope.uchicago.edu/Thayer/E/Roman/Texts/Cassius_Dio/62*.html

[29] The Hermetic texts can be read in translation at http://hermetic.com/texts/ and also http://gnosis.org/library/hermet.htm#CH

[30] See Lawrence M. Principe, *The Secrets of Alchemy*, Chicago, ILL: University of Chicago Press, 2013.

[31] Andrew M. T. Dibb, *Servetus, Swedenborg and the Nature of God*, University Press of America, 2005: 209.

[32] Karl Heinrich Ulrichs, 'Inclusa' 1864, in Magnus Hirschfeld, *Forschungen in der Ratsel des mannmannlichen Liebe*. Spohr, Leipzig, 1898.

[33] Pierre-Henri Castel, *La Métamorphose Impensable*, 413.

[34] Daniel Paul Schreber, *Memoirs of My Nervous Illness*, NY: New York Review of Books, 2000.

[35] Louis Sass, *Madness and Modernism: Insanity in the Light of Modern Art, Literature and Thought*, Cambridge, MA: Harvard University Press, 1994; Louis Sass, *The Paradoxes of Delusion: Wittgenstein, Schreber and the Schizophrenic Mind*, Ithaca, NY: Cornell University Press, 1995.

[36] http://en.m.wikipedia.org/wiki/Third_gender

[37] This argument is made in J. David Hester, 'Eunuchs and the Postgender Jesus: Matthew 19:12 and Transgressive Sexualities', *Journal for the Study of the New Testament*, 28(1) (2005)13-40.

[38] Within medicine, the term 'gender' was first used to denote a person's sense of being male or female by the English doctor William Blair Bell, founder of the Royal College of Obstetrics and Gynaecology. This was in the context of studying intersex conditions, not 'transgender' issues. William Blair Bell, 'Hermaphroditism', *Liverpool Medico-Chirurgical Journal* 35(1915)272-92. It was John Money who promoted the term through inventing the terms 'gender identity' and 'gender role'. John Money, Joan G. Hampson and John L. Hampson, 'Imprinting and the Establishment of Gender Role', *Archives of Neurology and Psychiatry* 77(1957)333-6. Robert Stoller first used the term in referring to a girl who wanted to be a boy. Robert Stoller, 'A contribution to the study of gender identity', *International Journal of Psychoanalysis* 45(1964)220-6.

[39] This topic has provoked a strong response from the Canadian academic psychologist Jordan B. Peterson due to the current Canadian Senate passing a Bill which would make 'gender identity' and 'gender expression' protected characteristics under non-discrimination and hate speech laws. See http://jordanbpeterson.com for updates.

[40] Tables can be found at http://www.comresglobal/com/polls/not-dead-yet-care-not-killing-assisted-suicide-poll/, published on 6 November 2014.

[41] Afua Hirsch, 'Trans People: Poll Reveals Changing Attitudes', 16 July, 2015. http://news.sky.com/story/trans-people-poll-reveals-changing-attitudes-10352288

[42] Amy Packham, 'Majority of British People would support their children if they wanted to change sex, survey reveals', Huffington Post UK, 14 December, 2015, http://www.huffingtonpost.co.uk/2015/12/14/transgender-children-support_n_8802930.html

[43] http://survation.com/uk-attitudes-to-gender-in-2016-survation-for-fawcett-society/

[44] Az Hakeem, 'Trans-sexuality: A case of "The Emperor's New Clothes", in David Morgan and Stanley Ruszczynski (eds.), *Lectures on Violence, Perversion and Delinquency*, London: Karnac Books, 2007.

[45] Colette Chiland, *Transsexualism: Illusion and Reality*, London: Continuum, 2003, 153.

2

GENDER DYSPHORIA

DR RICK THOMAS AND DR PETER SAUNDERS

Changing views of transsexuality are making waves in popular culture, politics and medicine. This chapter examines these developments from a Christian and scientific perspective and will be of interest to health professionals, pastors, churches, organisations and families relating to people with gender dysphoria (previously gender identity disorder).[1]

Bruce Jenner, American Olympic gold medal-winning decathlete, made headline news in 2015 when he publicly announced his transition to a female, Caitlyn Jenner. In 2016, nominations for BAFTA awards included *The Danish Girl*, a film loosely based on the life of Einar Wegener, a Dutch painter in the 1920s who transitioned to Lili Elbe and became one of the first to undergo reassignment surgery, from the complications of which she tragically died.

Transgender people – those who identify with a different gender to the one assigned to them at birth – were first given legal recognition in their new gender under the terms of the UK Gender Recognition Act 2004.[2] To acquire Gender Recognition Certificates they had to have been medically diagnosed with significant dysphoria (discomfort or distress as a result of a mismatch between their biological sex and gender identity[3]) and to have lived successfully for at least two years whilst presenting themselves in their acquired gender.

The Equality Act 2010[4] made it unlawful to discriminate against transgender people and the Marriage (Same Sex Couples) Act 2013[5] made it possible for an opposite-sex marriage to continue following one partner's gender transition, given the agreement of the other.

A recent parliamentary committee report called for a move away from viewing transgender identity as a disease or disorder of the mind, and replacement of the present medicalised process with a simplified administrative procedure based on self declaration by the individual applicant, free of intrusion by medical and legal personnel. The same report proposed that 16- and 17- year-olds should be eligible to apply for gender recognition, that children should be able to use puberty-blockers and cross-sex hormones earlier, and that Government should move towards 'non-gendering' official records.[6]

Changes in the law reflect changes in public attitudes and culture and have their counterparts in professional guidelines. The US Diagnostic and Statistical Manual of Mental Disorders, Fourth Edition (DSM-4, 1994) referred to cross-gender identification as 'Gender Identity Disorder'.[7] In the Fifth Edition (DSM-5, 2013)[8] the same phenomenon is described as 'Gender Dysphoria', shifting the emphasis from gender incongruence as a disorder to the distress (dysphoria) associated with the experience of that incongruence: 'It is important to note that gender nonconformity is not in itself a mental disorder. The critical element of gender dysphoria is the presence of clinically significant distress associated with the condition'.[9]

This change appears to have been ideologically driven, the aim being to de-pathologise gender incongruence. A minority of psychologists and psychiatrists dispute the reclassification, preferring to see gender identity disorder as a body image disorder whereby a person may have an unshakeable conviction that they are one gender when in fact they are the other.

The General Medical Council (GMC) has produced guidance for doctors treating transgender patients[10] and the Royal College of Psychiatrists published its 'UK Good Practice Guidelines' in 2013.[11]

Sex and Gender

For almost 400 years Western societies have embraced a scientific understanding of the world, based on physical observations. Thus, at birth, a child's sex is determined by examining its external genitalia. Genetically, males have XY sex chromosomes and females XX; morphologically, males have testes and females have ovaries. Biochemically, sex hormones such as testosterone (male) and oestrogen (female) trigger the appearance of secondary sex characteristics (eg. voice, body hair distribution, menstruation).

This observed 'binary' system fits with the biblical description of created humanity as male and female.[12] Very rarely a person is born with an intersex condition,[13] when it may be very difficult to determine the sex due to abnormalities in hormonal function or chromosomes. These conditions reflect disorders of sexual differentiation in the developing embryo and do not represent a 'third sex'. They should not be confused with transsexual people whose biological sex is not in doubt but who feel emotionally and psychologically as if they were born into the 'wrong' body. Most people experience congruence between their biological sex and their sense of gender identity, but for some people that congruence is lacking, sometimes from an early age, and they experience a degree of distress, or 'dysphoria', as a result.

Traditionally, the terms 'sex' and 'gender' have been clearly distinguished, 'sex' referring to a person's biological make-up and 'gender' to those roles and behaviours typically associated with masculinity and femininity. Stereotypical gender roles may always have been in part generalisations, but in any case they have not survived recent changes in culture. Increasingly, gender is being seen as a social construct, even a matter of choice.[14] Gender identity is being portrayed as 'fluid' rather than fixed, a fluctuating point along a continuum of possible experience between male and female that may encompass aspects of both.[15] 'Transgender' is the umbrella term used for the various ways in which people might live out their gender identities, outside of the simple categories of male and female.

Ways of viewing Gender Identity concerns

Mark Yarhouse,[16] a clinical psychologist, describes three different lenses through which people may view gender identity concerns:[17]

1. *The integrity framework*

This view emphasises the sacred integrity of maleness and femaleness in creation, and the importance of their complementarity. One's biological sex is an immutable and essential aspect of one's personhood and to tamper with it is a denial of something sacred.

2. *The disability framework*

This view recognises the fallen nature of our world and sees gender dysphoria as an example of things not being the way they were meant to be. It portrays dysphoria not as an immoral choice but as a non-moral, mental health disability in which sex and gender are not in alignment, to be addressed with compassion.

3. *The diversity framework*

In this view transgender issues are seen as something to be celebrated and honoured as part of normal human diversity. Its more strident proponents wish to blur the distinctions between sex and gender, recasting both as outdated social constructs.

In our Western cultural context, the diversity framework is emerging as most salient and is the view that increasingly drives public policy agendas. It is also becoming the prevailing source of guidance within the mental health professions. As a step towards the development of a nuanced Christian response to inform practice, pastoral care and public policy engagement, Yarhouse suggests an *integrated framework* for understanding gender incongruence that includes:

- respect for the integrity of sex differences
- empathy and compassion in the management of gender dysphoria
- identity, community and meaning for those navigating gender dysphoric lives

What are the causes of Gender Dysphoria?

Prevalence studies conclude that fewer than 1 in 10,000 adult natal males and 1 in 30,000 adult natal females meet the criteria for gender dysphoria, but such estimates vary widely.[18] Gender dysphoria in adults is associated with an elevated prevalence of comorbid psychopathology, especially mood disorders, anxiety disorders, and suicidality.[19] Mechanisms are incompletely understood, but genetic, neurodevelopmental, and psychosocial factors probably all contribute. Various theories exist and, as in the debate about homosexuality, their proponents tend to favour either nature or nurture explanations.

Most popular among those who believe nature is making the significant contribution is the brain-sex theory, referring to ways in which brain structure scripts towards male or female dispositions or behaviours.[20] But cohort sizes in cited studies are very small, post-mortem samples often come from transsexual persons who had used hormone treatments, and studies focus on brain morphology to the exclusion of other considerations like brain connectivity, load and efficiency. To the unbiased observer, results are highly inconclusive.[21]

Proponents of theories that suggest nurture makes the significant contribution give greater weight to the psychosocial environment in childhood.[22] But cited studies tend to be correlational in design and although they may point to a relationship between gender identity struggles and psychosocial factors, they do not prove causation.

Given the breadth of the transgender umbrella, one unifying theory that would account for development seems unlikely. It may well be that aetiology is multifactorial and that contributions come from both nature and nurture. Good research, unbiased interpretation, open discussion and humility are all to be desired in seeking greater understanding. What does seem to emerge from clinical experience is that 'true' gender dysphoria is not 'chosen'.[23] It is isolating and distressing and sometimes the dysphoria may be compounded by hostility from others or by social stigma. With changing societal attitudes towards transgender people, those with 'true' dysphoria may be being supplemented by others who are confused or experimental, but without more research it is not possible to be sure.

Approaches to Treatment

Should greater weight be given to a person's gender identity so as to alter their body to conform to that identity (through hormones or transgender surgery), or should a person experiencing gender dysphoria receive psychological treatment or counselling aimed at altering their sense of gender identity to conform to their biology? Or should they simply be supported in their contradictory state?

As our culture moves towards a diversity framework, the notion of gender fluidity is increasingly accepted and the idea of trying to 'correct' a person's gender identity to conform to their biological sex is correspondingly less acceptable. Political correctness about the new orthodoxy can be strongly expressed and it is becoming increasingly difficult publicly to state alternative (and previously widely held) views.[24]

(a) Children

Questions about whether and how to treat children who present with gender dysphoria are particularly contentious. Some children seem naturally to go through a temporary phase of wanting to be the other sex and to dress in other clothes, but appear to 'grow out of it' just as naturally and go on to develop a congruent gender identity. According to the DSM-5, rates of persistence of gender dysphoria from childhood into adolescence or adulthood vary. In biological males, persistence has ranged from 2 to 30 percent. In biological females, persistence has ranged from 12 to 50 percent.[25] It is clear that, for the majority of gender-confused boys and girls, gender dysphoria desists over time as they enter adolescence,[26] though a significant proportion of them go on to identify as bi-sexual or same-sex attracted (ranging from 63 to 100 percent for biological males, and 32 to 50 percent for biological females).[27]

For those children whose dysphoria does not desist naturally, there are several treatment options that have been recommended by various therapists:

1. 'Watchful waiting' approach – in which cross-gender behaviour is permitted but not encouraged.[28] This approach allows a child to explore various gender activities without the imposition of rigid gender stereotypes and allows the

child to gravitate towards his or her own interests.

2. Intervention to decrease cross-gender identification, using behavioural therapy approaches – coaching parents to ignore cross-sex behaviour and to encourage gender-appropriate activities and play, and psychotherapeutic approaches – aimed at intervening more 'within' the child. In this way, the majority of children who are gender dysphoric experience resolution of their dysphoria before adolescence.[29] However, it is not known what proportion would have resolved 'naturally' and what proportion responded to intervention. The Portman Clinic[30] in London reported that 80 percent of children referred for gender dysphoria chose as adults to maintain a gender identity consistent with their birth sex.[31] Further research is needed.

3. Facilitating social transition to the other gender by using affirmative approaches, for example the adoption of a new name, preferred gender hairstyle, clothing and play.[32]

4. Puberty Suppression. Children between the ages of 10 and 13 are given monthly injections of hypothalamic hormone blockers, thus preventing the gonads from making oestrogen and testosterone, in order to delay puberty and allow time for the gender-conflicted child to enter adolescence and make a more mature decision (at around the age of 16) whether to affirm either their birth sex or their cross-gender identity. If the latter, then they begin taking the hormones of the opposite sex.

Given that dysphoria will desist naturally without active intervention in the majority of children as puberty progresses, there should be no rush to facilitate early social transition or puberty suppression. There are additional concerns with puberty suppression about brain development, bone growth and subfertility, as well as the possibility that the dysphoria might naturally have abated at the age of 12 or 13, but by which time treatment would have commenced.[33]

(b) Adults

The Standards of Care of the World Professional Association for Transgender Health (WPATH) note that the primary goal of therapy is 'to find ways to maximise a person's overall psychological well-being, quality of life and self-fulfilment'.[34] In general, the least invasive treatment option that enables the patient to live with, or find relief from, dysphoria is recommended by clinicians as the treatment of choice.

Treatment outcomes in adults point to a high attrition rate with as many as 50 percent of those who seek services dropping out due to personal ambivalence or frustration with the length, complexity or cost of the process.[35] It is not clear what happens to these people, but it seems likely that they find a way to compartmentalise their dysphoria, sufficiently to be able to function in life, or come to accept their biological sex and gender role.[36]

Of those who undergo psychological treatment towards resolution in favour of their birth sex, a majority do not report resolution.[37] Instead, the most frequent outcome is to engage in cross-gender behaviours intermittently, often privately or in distant locales, as a coping strategy to reduce the felt tension within.[38]

Finally, there are those who adopt full-time the gender role of the opposite sex. This may or may not involve having hormone treatment and/or reassignment surgery[39] following a psychological assessment and a period living full-time in the acquired gender.

Research on the outcome of gender reassignment surgery indicates that for the majority (about 75 per cent) of those who undergo this process, the outcome is positive.[40] Predictors of a good outcome include good pre-reassignment psychological adjustment, family support, at least one year of living in the desired role, consistent use of hormones and previous psychological treatment. The author points to implications of the research that include an appreciation of the diversity of transgendered experience, the need for more research on non-reassignment resolutions to gender dysphoria, and the importance of assisting the transgendered individual to identify the resolution that best suits him or her.

A more recent review of over 300 people who completed sex-reassignment surgery in Sweden over a fifty year period reported high levels of satisfaction and low levels (2.2 per cent) of regret,[41] but also considerably higher risks for mortality, suicidal behaviour, and psychiatric morbidity than the general population.[42] The long term study reveals only that there is an association between reassignment surgery and increased suicide risk in later life; it does not prove causation.

Commenting on the review, former Johns Hopkins chief psychiatrist Paul McHugh noted that the suicide mortality amongst those who had had sex reassignment surgery rose almost 20-fold above the comparable non-transgender population – a disturbing result that he felt might reflect the growing sense of isolation reported by aging transgendered people after surgery.[43] He suggests that psychiatry has caved in to individual preferences and cultural pressures, and likens sex-reassignment surgery to 'liposuction on anorexics'.[44] In the US, suicide attempts among trans men (46%) and trans women (42%) are roughly ten times the rate found in the overall population, according to the findings of the US National Transgender Discrimination Survey.[45] Researchers found a number of factors that influenced whether a person was more likely to attempt suicide – in short, the more forms of discrimination, harrassment and victimisation that transgender people experienced, the more likely they were to attempt suicide. A recent study from Ontario confirms this effect. There, the suicide attempt rate for transgender people was about 18 times higher than the general population, but the study also found that some factors greatly reduced the attempt rate. In particular, the closer they were to having a body and outward identity that matched their internal gender identity, the less likely they were to attempt suicide.[46]

Studies investigating the prevalence of psychiatric disorders among transgender people have identified elevated rates of psychopathology. A recent review[47] identified 38 cross-sectional and longitudinal studies describing prevalence rates of psychiatric disorders and psychiatric outcomes, pre- and post-gender-confirming medical interventions, for people with gender dysphoria. It indicated that, although the levels of psychopathology and psychiatric disorders (mainly depression and anxiety) in transgender people attending services at the time of assessment are higher than in the non-trans population, they do improve following gender-confirming medical intervention, in many cases reaching normative values. However, there was conflicting evidence regarding gender differences and many studies were methodologically weak. For example, those who progress as far as medical intervention are (because of screening) the most psychologically stable. Perhaps this indicates the difficulty of scientific objectivity in an area where there are so many vested interests.

Current GMC guidance permits a doctor 'not to provide or refer any patients (including patients proposing to undergo gender reassignment) for particular services to which he or she may hold a conscientious objection'.[48, 49]

There are some very practical concerns that result from legislation that recognises gender-reassignment. Changing legal identity does not change biological identity. In aspects of health care, it is important to know a person's biological sex. Some people prefer to see a woman doctor and may feel intimidated or uncomfortable if that doctor were to be transsexual. Sports organisations want to be sure that those competing in women's events do so 'on a level playing field'. Which changing rooms and toilets should transsexual people use? The situation is more complex still if they have changed legal gender but had no hormonal and/or surgical intervention.

Gender dysphoria represents a mismatch between a person's perception of their gender and their actual biological sex. The danger is that in giving so much attention to changing a person's body to bring the two in line, not enough effort will be given to helping the person alter their gender perception to fit their biological sex, which will remain unaltered by surgery.

The status given by Western society to self-designation and individual choice, and the belief that technology can enable us to transform or escape what in the past was a given but may be experienced as a negative even destructive limitation, combine to empower the view that gender identity should take priority over biological sex.

The Bible and Sexuality

The Bible teaches that God made human beings in his image and of two sexes – 'male and female he created them'.[50] They are different by design, but equal in value and, as St Paul makes clear (cf. Galatians 3:28), enjoy equal access to God's grace. God gave human beings a 'stewardship' mandate to multiply and fill the earth[51] and equipped them with complementary bodies in order to fulfil that plan. In uniting as man and wife they would become 'one flesh'[52] and the Apostle Paul teaches us that this exclusive and loving union would be an 'icon', or sign of the love and union of Jesus and his bride, the Church.[53]

In a discussion with his disciples about marriage and divorce, Jesus refers to three kinds of 'eunuchs' – those able to live contentedly as single persons.[54] He includes those 'born as eunuchs' – recognising that a fallen world may include what we now call 'disorders of sexual development' – and those 'who have made themselves eunuchs for the sake of the kingdom of heaven' – Jesus appears to celebrate those who have set aside their freedom to marry to serve His kingdom, a theme picked up by Paul when writing to the church in Corinth.[55]

Whilst Christians may have a range of views about gender role stereotypes, they do hold to a binary view of gender as God's created pattern and must resist the redefinition of gender as fluid.

The Bible makes no specific mention of transsexuality; but the warning against 'cross-dressing'[56] could perhaps best be understood in context as a comment upon actions aimed at blurring or confusing the clear gender distinctions within created design. The reference to the ritual uncleanness of those with testicular injury[57] may also have relevance for surgical procedures aimed at altering normal external genitalia.

Christians acknowledge that, as a result of the Fall, things are no longer as they were meant to be. The knowledge of God is scarce, and his pattern for human flourishing is unknown or ignored by many. The Fall distorts 'both the physical experiences and the cultural expressions of gender'.[58] But the good news at the heart of the Christian message is that God is a redeemer, graciously restoring something of his marred image in those who turn to him, and working through them lovingly to restore something of the brokenness in society. Ultimately, his promise is that all of creation will be fully restored in the new heaven and new earth,[59] but for now we are individual 'works in progress' as the Holy Spirit continues to make us more and more like Jesus Christ.

Christians should be careful not to adopt a legalistic

and simplistic stance, representing the choice faced by the gender dysphoric person in terms of a simple yes/no decision of the will, for or against obedience to God's law. We do better to recognise the confusing complexity of the conflict being experienced, offering acceptance, community and compassion in working with the person to find the least invasive ways to manage the dysphoria, all the time pointing them to the One in whose image they are made and in whom wholeness is found.

To those wrestling with gender confliction and in-congruence, as with all disorders, the gospel brings hope that the God who made us male and female can realign distorted identity and bring increasing coherence between sex and gender, even if such healing may not always be fully realised in this life.

Toward a Christian response
Christians must ensure that marginalised minorities are protected. Therefore they will strongly endorse the human rights of transgender people, affirming their dignity and guarding them from discrimination.

Many transsexual people experience profound loneliness, sometimes aggravated by the shame and rejection they often feel projected towards them by religious people. By offering true friendship and acceptance, Christians can help transform the experience of those isolated by their dysphoria.

True gender dysphoria is not a wilful choice, not deliberate sin. Very few transgender people are intent on deconstructing meaningful categories of sex and gender. Compassion and empathy should characterise a pastoral response. Whilst clearly teaching the truth to all age groups, that God made mankind in his own image, male and female, Christians must find ways of helping gender-conflicted people experience welcome, identity and community amongst them, discovering for themselves a relationship with God, the transforming power of his loving fatherhood and the wisdom of his ways. The presence in churches of such transgender people, seeking to navigate their way as disciples of Jesus with integrity amidst complexity, is surely to be welcomed. It is an approach that chimes with Yarhouse's suggestion of an 'integrated framework' described above.

Beyond that, it may become possible to encourage a person with gender dysphoria to consider strategies to resolve their dysphoria in line with their birth sex. However, where those coping strategies appear to be unsuccessful, some people may then choose to seek relief from their dysphoria through crossgender identity behaviour, hormone treatment, and even sex reassignment surgery. However, less radical and permanent strategies – rather than pharmacological or surgical intervention – will be preferable.

A merciful, compassionate Christian response will involve continuing to care for people whatever choices that they make, even when they resort to more drastic strategies in an attempt to cope with their dysphoria. However, continuing to provide care should not imply endorsement of such choices as morally right or clinically appropriate, and many Christian clinicians will refuse to refer patients to gender reassignment on conscience grounds, believing that it cannot be in their patients' best interests to embark on strategies that disregard God's pattern in creation.

Conforming to the Lordship of Christ means seeking God's grace and strength neither to surrender to our felt passions and inclinations if they cause us to act contrary to divinely ordained patterns, nor to encourage or assist others to do so.

'Wholeness' is found in relationship with God, and in following his ways and wisdom. Each of us is called to walk in obedience as a disciple of Christ, regardless of the cost to us personally, just as when a Christian who experiences strong feelings of same-sex erotic attraction chooses not to express them but rather to live a life of faithfulness and celibacy.

Our identity as Christians is not in our felt gender but in Christ, whether male, female, intersex or gender conflicted. In the words of John Wyatt, we are 'flawed masterpieces'[60] undergoing restoration in the present and with a glorious future to come.

Terms

Transgender
An umbrella term for the many ways in which people might experience and/or live out their gender identities differently from people whose sense of gender identity is congruent with their biological sex

Intersex
A term that describes conditions in which a person is born with ambiguous sex characteristics or anatomy – chromosomal, gonadal or genital

Gender Dysphoria
The experience of distress associated with incongruence between one's biological sex and one's psychological and emotional gender identity. The degree of dysphoria and the effectiveness of coping strategies vary from person to person

Transsexual
A person who has concluded that he/she was born in the 'wrong' body and wishes to transition (or already has transitioned) through hormone treatment and/or reassignment surgery

Genderfluid
A term used by a person who wishes to convey that their experience of gender is not fixed as male or female, but may fluctuate along a continuum and/or encompass aspects of both gender identities

Gender bending
Intentionally crossing, or 'bending' gender roles

Cross-dressing
Dressing in the clothing, or adopting a presentation, of the other sex. Motivations vary

Transvestism

Dressing or adopting the presentation of the other sex, often for the purpose of sexual arousal. Not generally associated with gender dysphoria and may not identify as transgender.

Notes

[1] Sims A. Gender Identity Disorder. *CMF Files* 2004;25 *bit.ly/1SnAlrT*

[2] Gender Recognition Act 2004. *Legislation.gov.uk bit.ly/1TUuFMC*

[3] Gender Dysphoria. *NHS Choices*. 29 April 2014 *bit.ly/1XrXvmV*

[4] Equality Act 2010. Legislation.gov.uk *bit.ly/1k8a7wN*

[5] Marriage (Same Sex Couples) Act 2013. Legislation.gov.uk *bit.ly/147SGIV*

[6] *Transgender Equality: First Report of Session 2015-16*. House of Commons Women and Equalities Committee, 8 December 2015

[7] DSM-4. American Psychiatric Association, *Diagnostic and Statistical Manual of Mental Disorders*, 4th edn. Washington DC: American Psychiatric Publishing, 1994:576

[8] DSM-5. American Psychiatric Association, *Diagnostic and Statistical Manual of Mental Disorders*, 5th edn. Washington DC: American Psychiatric Publishing, 2013 *bit.ly/21rkCho*

[9] *Gender Dysphoria Fact Sheet*. American Psychiatric Association, 2013 *bit.ly/XB7v3T*

[10] Guidance for doctors treating transgender patients. *General Medical Council*, 2016 *bit.ly/1SOhxYI*

[11] *UK Good Practice Guidelines For The Assessment And Treatment Of Adults With Gender Dysphoria*. RCPsych Report CR181, October 2013 *bit.ly/1RKs66Hh*

[12] Genesis 1:27

[13] Intersex conditions include sex chromosome combinations that are neither XX nor XY (eg. XO, XXX, XXY, XYY), structural abnormalities (eg. Poorly developed or absent vagina, gonadal dysgenesis) or abnormalities of hormonal function (eg. Congenital adrenal hyperplasia, androgen insensitivity syndrome).

[14] Butler J. *Gender Trouble: Feminism and the Subversion of Identity*. New York: Routledge; 1990:7

[15] International Gay and Lesbian Human Rights Commission, Institutional memoir of the 2005 Institute for Trans and Intersex Activist Training, 2005:7-8.

[16] Yarhouse M. *Understanding Gender Dysphoria*. IVP Academic: Illinois; 2015:20-21

[17] Ibid: 46-57

[18] Zucker KJ et al. Gender Dysphoria in Adults. *Annu Rev Clin Psychol* 2016 (18 January Epub ahead of print).

[19] Zucker KJ, Ibid.

[20] Zhou JN et al. A sex difference in the human brain and its relation to transsexuality. *Nature*; 1995; 378:68-70

[21] Bailey M, Triea K. What many transgender activists don't want you to know. *Perspectives in Biology and Medicine*, 2007; 50(4):521-534

[22] Meyer-Bahlburg HF. Gender Identity Disorder in young boys: a parent- and peer-based treatment protocol. *Clinical Child Psychology and Psychiatry*, 2002; 7(3):360-76

[23] Yarhouse M. *Understanding Gender Dysphoria*, p.81

[24] At the time of writing, even the feminist icon Germain Greer has been branded 'trans-phobic' and has been 'no-platformed'(denied invitations to speak) at British universities for suggesting that men who have had gender-reassignment surgery are not 'real women'. *Independent*, 26 October 2015.

[25] DSM-5. American Psychiatric Association, *Diagnostic and Statistical Manual of Mental Disorders*, 5th edn. Washington DC: American Psychiatric Publishing, 2013, 302.85:455

[26] Zucker KJ. Measurement of psychosexual differentiation. *Arch Sex Behav* 2005;34(4):375-388

[27] DSM-5, 2013:302.85:455

[28] De Vries A L C and Cohen-Ketennis PT. *Clinical Management of Gender Dysphoria in Children and Adolescents: The Dutch Approach*, 2012:309

[29] Meyer-Bahlberg HLF. *Op Cit.* pp360-76

[30] The Portman Clinic offers specialised long-term psychoanalytic psychotherapeutic help to people who suffer from problems arising from delinquent, criminal or violent behaviour or from disturbing and damaging sexual behaviours or experiences.

[31] Spiegel A. Parents consider treatment to delay son's puberty. *National Public Radio*, 8 May 2008

[32] Olson J et al. Management of the transgender adolescent. *Archives of Paediatrics and Adolescent Medicine* 2011;165 (2):173

[33] Kreukels BP and Cohen-Kettenis PT. Puberty Suppression in Gender Identity Disorder: The Amsterdam Experience, *National Review of Endocrinology*, 2011;17(7):466-72

[34] Colman E et al. WPATH – Standards of Care for the Health of Transsexual, Transgender, and Gender-Nonconforming People, Version 7, *International Journal of Transgenderism*, 2011;13:165-232

[35] Carroll R. Gender dysphoria and transgender experiences, in *Principles and Practice of Sex Therapy*, 4th edn, ed. Leiblum SR. New York: Guilford; 2007:490

[36] Yarhouse M. *Understanding Gender Dysphoria*, p112

[37] Carroll R. Gender dysphoria and transgender experiences, p491

[38] Ibid

[39] Some prefer the term 'gender-affirming surgery'. A range of surgical procedures is available and not all those who have such procedures

will pursue the full range. They may carry significant medical and psychological risk and cost.

[40] Carroll R. Outcomes of Treatment for Gender Dysphoria. *Journal of Sex Education and Therapy*, 1999; 24(3):128-136

[41] Dhejne C et al. An analysis of all applications for sex reassignment surgery in Sweden, 1960-2010: Prevalence, incidence and regrets. *Archives of Sexual Behaviour* 2014; 43, 8:1535-45

[42] Dhejne C et al. Long-Term Follow-Up of Transsexual Persons Undergoing Sex Reassignment Surgery: Cohort Study in Sweden. *PLoS One* 2011; 6(2): e16885 doi: 10.1371/journal.pone.0016885

[43] McHugh P. Transgender surgery isn't the solution. *The Wall Street Journal*, June 12, 2014.

[44] McHugh P. Psychiatric Misadventures. *American Scholar* 1992;61(4): 503.

[45] Haas AP et al. Suicide attempts among transgender and gender non-conforming adults: Findings from the National Transgender Discrimination Survey. *bit.ly/1n7HXBJ*

[46] Bauer G et al. Intervenable factors associated with suicide risk in transgender persons: a respondent driven sampling study in Ontario, Canada. *BMC Public Health*, 2015;15:525

[47] Dhejne C et al. Mental health and gender dysphoria: A review of the literature. *Int Rev Psychiatry* 2016; 28(1):44-57

[48] Conscientious objection. *Good Medical Practice*. GMC, 2013

[49] Wyatt J. The doctor's conscience. *CMF Files* 2009; 39 *bit.ly/1U17hOP*

[50] Genesis 1:27

[51] Genesis 1:28

[52] Genesis 2:24

[53] Ephesians 5:32

[54] Matthew 19:11

[55] 1 Corinthians 7:7

[56] Deuteronomy 22:5

[57] Deuteronomy 23:1

[58] Looy H, Bouma H. The Nature of Gender: Gender identity in persons who are intersexed or transgendered. *J Psych and Theo* 2005; 33(3):176

[59] Romans 8:19-23; 2 Corinthians 5:1-5; Philippians 3:20, 21; Revelation 21:1-4

[60] Wyatt J. *Matters of Life and Death*, Nottingham: IVP, 2009:120

3

CHILDREN, SEX REASSIGNMENT SURGERY, AND THE AIMS OF MEDICINE

Carlos D. Flores

The issue of transgenderism that seems to have burst into the scene a year or so ago has gone from something that can be dismissed with a laugh to something that, if not taken seriously, can lead to one's incarceration. From compulsory use of 'preferred gender pronouns' to compulsory insurance coverage of sex reassignment surgery, the transgender agenda is bringing its weight to bear on the social order of the West.

Advocates of transgenderism, however, almost never realise that transgenderism rests on highly implausible assumptions about medicine, ethics, and the nature of the human person. The advocate of transgenderism seems to hold, for example, to the following theses:

1. That sex reassignment surgery (SRS) is a perfectly proper procedure of medicine.

2. That procuring and providing sex reassignment surgery is, all things considered, morally permissible.

3. That attempts to relieve transgenderism through pejoratively labelled 'conversion therapy' (i) are not proper procedures of medicine and (ii) are morally impermissible.

4. That children can permissibly be given sex reassignment surgery or hormonal treatment to prepare them for sex reassignment surgery in the future.

In this essay, I want to call into question these theses.

Teleology and the Human Body

Let us begin by noting (and providing an argument for) an assumption that is crucial for the aims of this chapter. The assumption is this: that our bodily faculties are inherently *oriented towards* achieving certain ends. This is to say that bodily faculties have *natural* and *inherent* functions. At first glance, this seems obvious. Here we can, for the moment, leave inference and argument aside and simply ask ourselves: is the heart not *oriented towards* pumping blood? Is the eye not *oriented towards* seeing? To ask these questions, it seems, is to answer them—the heart *is* oriented towards pumping blood; the eye *is* oriented towards seeing.

To be sure, however, it can be demonstrated that at least some of our faculties really are oriented towards ends. To see this, consider our mental faculties. Our mental faculties, it turns out, are, like our bodily faculties, oriented towards certain ends as well. Among these ends is the attainment of truth. Yet it seems that one can only deny that our mental faculties are oriented towards attaining truth on pain of self-refutation. For in denying that our mental faculties are oriented towards attaining truth, one is, in effect, implicitly saying that his mental faculties are grasping a truth, namely, that 'our mental faculties are not oriented towards attaining truth'. Thus, one who denies this claim implicitly affirms it.

What is Health?

Consider now the question of what health is. As Dr. Leon Kass elegantly puts it, 'medicine is an art which aims at health.'[1] And health is the proper functioning of bodily faculties.

This is simple enough to see when we consider bodily faculties in isolation: a healthy eye is one that sees well, healthy lungs are those that respire well, and healthy hearts are those which pump blood well. But one should also speak of health as not merely the proper functioning of a particular bodily faculty but as the proper functioning of the human organism *considered as a whole*. Thus, a healthy person is one whose parts function well in unison towards the end of the bodily life of the whole. Of course, it bears noting that bodily health is necessary but not sufficient for the holistic flourishing of the human person.

What is Medicine?

Consider now the question of what medicine is. In order to know what medicine is not, one needs to know what medicine *is*. The following cases should help us to grasp what medicine is.

Case 1: A man whose eyesight has recently worsened visits an ophthalmologist to see what is the matter with his eye. The doctor identifies the problem with his eye and restores the man's eye to its proper function.

Case 2: A physician giving his patient a routine check-up notices that, if left untreated, his patient's cholesterol levels will kill him by way of cardiac arrest. The doctor recommends that his patient change his diet, and he prescribes cholesterol-reducing medication and physical exercise. The recommendations are efficacious in reducing the patient's cholesterol levels.

Case 3: A woman books an appointment with a plastic surgeon because she believes that her nose is aesthetically displeasing. There is nothing functionally wrong with her nose—she can breathe comfortably and easily detect different smells. The surgeon proceeds to remove some cartilage from her nose to mould it into a more aesthetically pleasing shape.

Case 4: A man with perfectly functioning arms desires to have one of his arms removed. In his opinion, doing so would allow him to truly 'be himself' and to 'be more comfortable' in his own body. Besides the desire to remove his arm, the man seems perfectly reasonable. The man books an appointment with a surgeon and the surgeon agrees to remove the man's arm.

The first two cases seem quite clearly to be medical procedures. The third case is questionable. The fourth example certainly does not qualify as medicine.

The first two cases reveal important truths about medicine. First, medicine *restores bodily faculties to their proper function*. Second, medicine *prevents the dysfunction of bodily faculties*.

Indeed, this simply is the account of medicine that has prevailed for thousands of years in the Western tradition and which explains the content and spirit of the Hippocratic Oath, particularly its *primum non nocere* (first, do no harm) maxim. Call this account of medicine, then, the Hippocratic account.

Our hesitance to consider the third case a medical procedure is explained by the fact that the procedure is not oriented towards either the restoring of a bodily faculty to its proper function or to preventing a bodily faculty's dysfunction. But notice that our intuitions don't seem to go further than this; our intuitions tell us that the third procedure is not a medical one, but our intuitions do not seem to tell us that it is *contrary* to medicine.

In the fourth case, however, rather than being oriented towards the restoring of a faculty to its proper function or preventing its dysfunction, the procedure *intentionally* frustrates and damages bodily faculties. Because of this, we can say something much stronger about the fourth case: *it is contrary to the aims of medicine*.

And so, this account of medicine seems to aptly explain our intuition that Case 1 is a medical procedure: Case 1 involves a perfectly proper procedure of medicine insofar as the ophthalmologist undertakes an activity that is oriented towards the restoring of a bodily faculty to its proper function. This account of medicine seems to aptly explain our intuition that Case 2 is a medical procedure: Case 2 involves a perfectly proper procedure of medicine insofar as the doctor undertakes an activity that is oriented towards preventing the dysfunction of bodily faculties.

This account of medicine seems to aptly explain our reluctance to say that Case 3 is a medical procedure: to the extent that the procedure undertaken in Case 3 is not oriented towards restoring a bodily faculty to its proper function and/ or the preventing of dysfunction of any bodily faculty, such a procedure—whatever sort of procedure it might be—is not a medical procedure. Finally, this account of medicine aptly explains our intuition that Case 4 is not a medical procedure: Case 4 is not a medical procedure insofar as it is not oriented to the restoring of bodily faculties to their proper function and/or to preventing their dysfunction but is rather oriented towards the intentional damaging and injuring of bodily faculties. It is for this reason that Case 4 is not simply *not* medicine but is *positively contrary* to medicine.

Sex Reassignment Surgery (SRS) is not Medicine

We are prepared, then, to give an argument for why sex reassignment surgery is not medicine. Here is the argument:
Premise 1: If sex reassignment surgery is a medical procedure, then it is oriented towards either (i) the restoring of bodily (or mental) faculties to their proper function, or (ii) to the preventing of their dysfunction, or (iii) both.
Premise 2: Sex reassignment surgery is not oriented towards either (i) the restoring of bodily (or mental) faculties to their proper function, or (ii) to the preventing of their dysfunction, or (iii) both. Therefore, sex reassignment surgery is not a medical procedure.

Premise 1 has been defended in the previous section.

Whether premise 2 is true will depend upon empirical facts about SRS. However, premise 2 is straightforwardly true: SRS is a procedure that is undertaken with the aim of amputating or injuring bodily faculties.[2] Thus, SRS is not oriented towards restoring a bodily faculty to its proper function or to preventing its dysfunction. This suffices to show that SRS cannot, in principle, be a medical procedure.

Sex Reassignment Surgery is *Contrary* to Medicine

But one can make a stronger claim. Like Case 4, which is plainly contrary to the enterprise of medicine, SRS is a procedure whose object is to intentionally (and sometimes catastrophically) injure otherwise properly functioning bodily faculties and so it too is not merely not a medical procedure but is also contrary to the enterprise of medicine.

To be clear, the claim here is not that the mere presence of harm to bodily (or mental) faculties suffices to render a procedure a non-medical one, for the obvious reason that many procedures which we would have no problem describing as medical involve the damaging of bodily faculties, e.g. when a doctor creates an opening to a patient's badly-functioning heart to restore his heart to its proper function, damaging the patient's skin, flesh and bones that he has disturbed, foreseeably but unintentionally, to gain access to the heart in the process.

Rather, the claim is that sex reassignment surgery is *positively oriented towards the damaging, destruction, or removal of bodily faculties*. In the case where a doctor must open up someone's chest to reach his heart to restore it to its proper function, the doctor accepts as a proposal for action his restoring his patient's heart to its proper function and sees the damage to bodily faculties involved in this procedure as unintended side-effects of the procedure. On the other hand, in the case of SRS, the doctor accepts as a proposal for action the intentional damaging of the patient's bodily faculties, and the damage is not merely accepted as an unintended side effect.[3] This suffices to show that SRS is utterly contrary to the enterprise of medicine.

Consider what all of this in turn means for children. Since there are some transgenderism advocates who advocate that sex reassignment surgery be provided to children, what they are recommending for children is, in effect, a procedure that involves mutilation and is almost always irreversible. This seems to be a paradigmatic example of child abuse insofar as child abuse is, minimally, the intentional infliction of injury to a child.

Consider too that the much-maligned and pejoratively labelled 'conversion therapy' — that is, attempts by physicians and psychologists to restore a patient's understanding of his gender identity to accord with his physical sex — is, on the other hand, a perfectly proper procedure of medicine (despite attempts to ban it) insofar as it involves the restoring of a patient's mental faculties to their proper function by allowing the patient to recognise a truth about himself — that he is the sex that he is.

The fact that procedures such as these are so commonplace, coupled with the fact that we allow public persons to get away with calling such things medical procedures without challenging them, tells us that we have, to our fault, collectively lost a grasp of what medicine is and what it aims towards. Despite all the marvellous technological advances that have in many ways greatly benefited the enterprise of medicine, a perilous rot has set in to its philosophical foundations that is threatening to turn medicine, as it already has in part, from a noble art to an efficient servant of mutilation.

Medicine, in other words, is sickly, shambling, and begging to be treated. This is largely because we have for many decades neglected to care for it and allowed it to be treated as an instrument for sexual liberation and other political causes. It is a grave mistake, however—one that millions of dead unborn children and hundreds of regretful, mutilated persons can attest to — to pervert medicine for political goals. Because of this, we must invest in the project of restoring a proper understanding of medicine and the noble aim to which it tends: healthy and flourishing human bodies. For as Dr. Leon Kass warns, 'there will be an end *to* medicine unless there remains an end *for* medicine.'[4] We would be fools not to heed his warning.

Notes

[1] Kass, Leon R., *Regarding the End of Medicine and the Pursuit of Health*, *Public Interest*, 40 (1975: Summer).

[2] The truth of this is made very clear to anyone who has seen a sex reassignment procedure being conducted either in person or on video.

[3] This is easier to see if we consider the following: in the case of the doctor who is attempting to restore a patient's heart to its proper function, the doctor would be relieved if it were possible to restore the patient's heart to its proper function without causing any side-effect damage to the patient. It is impossible, on the other hand, for the surgeon who is to perform a sex reassignment procedure to separate the unintended damage from the carrying out of the sex reassignment procedure because the aim of modifying one's faculties to resemble faculties of the opposite sex (the goal of sex reassignment surgery) is inseparable from intentionally harming them.

[4] Kass, Leon R., *Regarding the End of Medicine and the Pursuit of Health*, *Public Interest*, 40 (1975: Summer).

TRANSSEXUAL AND TRANSGENDER RIGHTS AND IDEOLOGY IN THE UNITED KINGDOM: THEIR HISTORY AND EFFECT ON SOCIETY

Carys Moseley

The purpose of this chapter is to provide a general overview for the general reader of how transsexual/transgender rights and ideology developed in the United Kingdom and how they have affected society. The chapter will outline the origins and growth of the production of the category of transsexualism, the history of transsexual treatment and rights in the UK, variations in prevalence rates by country and the significance thereof, and highlight some issues regarding the relationship between transsexualism/transgenderism and mental health. Of necessity I cannot do justice in a short chapter to all matters raised; this would take a substantial book about what is a fast-changing subject.

The German origins of concept of transsexualism and migration of ideas to the USA

The whole field of the study of 'transsexualism' started in Germany during the time of Bismarck, and became popularised during the Weimar Republic.[1] In the late 19th century some medics specialising in the study of human sexuality started publishing cases of 'inversion', by which was meant people who claimed to feel as if they were of the opposite sex ('women trapped in men's bodies' and vice versa), and who acted on this. 'Inversion' in this sense tended to be associated at the time with homosexuality.

Eugen Steinach attempted transplantation on animals aimed at producing changes of sex. For example he castrated male rodents then implanted ovaries into them, thus feminising their behaviour. News of these experiments led some individuals on both sides of the Atlantic to request similar operations for themselves, predominantly men requesting castration and women requesting hysterectomies. The pioneer in the field, Magnus Hirschfeld coined the term 'Seelische Transsexualismus' (transsexualism of the soul) to refer to 'inversion'. He called people who wanted to change their sex 'transvestites'. Hirschfeld himself was gay and, like many liberally-minded medics of the time, an advocate of eugenics. Hirschfeld was invited to the United States in 1930 by Harry Benjamin, the American doctor whose successful campaigning for 'sex-change surgery' aimed to marginalise psychotherapeutic interventions for patients. Benjamin endorsed the view that a person's sex was defined by hormones, a definition which bypassed the more fundamental role of chromosomes and which conveniently justified administering artificial cross-sex hormones to transsexuals.[2] It was the American psychiatrist David O. Cauldwell who coined the meaning of 'transsexual' in English as referring to a person who wants to change their sex. Cauldwell refused to agree to 'sex-change' surgery for patients, stressing social factors in the genesis of the condition. Thus we can see that a definition and approach to transsexualism that favoured a psychological approach was born in the English-speaking world, in contrast to the biological and eugenic approach which was German-speaking. Nevertheless, the biological approach had also taken root in the USA and from the start was championed by the more socially libertarian doctors who believed in sexual emancipation and 'rights'. Benjamin became associated with Alfred Kinsey and shared research material on human sexuality, with the latter referring a male patient wishing to become a woman to him in 1949.

It was American medics who started to speak during the 1950s of adult transsexual patients' 'psychological sex', in the context of rejecting the notion that it was possible to change this to correspond with genetic sex.[3] This notion was taken up by John Money and his colleagues at the faculty of psychiatry in Johns Hopkins University when they started to use the term 'gender'. The argument was that intersexed children acquired their sense of being male or female from having been assigned to a particular sex at birth, and that attempting to modify gender later than early childhood was harmful.[4] The most notorious practical outworking of this dogma was the now infamous experiment that Money conducted on David Reimer. Reimer underwent a botched circumcision operation at eight months of age, and Money persuaded his parents to rear him as a girl instead, subjecting Reimer to sex reassignment surgery and psychological conditioning, in other words, brainwashing.[5] Reimer, however, later reported that he never considered himself a girl, was told that he was really a boy by his parents in his early teens and reverted to living as a boy at fifteen. Reimer also revealed that John Money had forced him and his twin brother to enact sexual experiments on each other, allegedly to prove the idea that sexual 'games' in childhood were good for healthy human development. Reimer suffered throughout his life despite returning to live as a male, and committed suicide at the age of 38. John Money is now dead, but has become notorious due to these experiments on children's sex and sexuality. In retrospect we should be very suspicious of his work as he had a link via Harry Benjamin to Alfred Kinsey, even more notorious for his sexual experimentation on children during the 1940s.[6]

With the rise of Hitler to power in Germany, the Nazi regime burnt down Hirschfeld's extensive archival material on sexual minorities, the *Institut fur Geschlechtswissenschaft*, allegedly because it contained so much incriminating evidence about the sexual tendencies of prominent Nazis. Transgender activists tend to omit the next stage in history, which is that 'sex-change' surgery was continued throughout the Nazi period, indeed it was alleged to have become more common, and that it was performed by Josef Mengele 'the Angel of Death' in the concentration camp in Auschwitz, where he performed forced operations on boys.[7] Like many other Nazis Mengele escaped to Argentina at the end of the Second World War. The State of Israel hunted for him in the early 1960s at the same time as Adolf Eichmann, but for various reasons did not catch him.[8] Had he been caught, he would have been taken to Jerusalem and tried for crimes against humanity, and perhaps 'sex-change operations' would have come to be seen as a crime against humanity. The fact that they are not is worth pondering in light of the very serious threat to health, welfare and freedom of speech that the transgender movement now poses across the western world, including the supplanting of the category of sex in law by that of 'gender', thus leading to diminishing protections for single-sex spaces, facilities and services for women and girls.[9]

Early history of transsexualism in the United Kingdom

John Randell was the original psychiatrist at Charing Cross who dealt with transvestites and transsexuals. He was appointed Physician for Psychological Medicine at Charing Cross on 1 January 1950. He died on 23 April 1982.[10] Randell started his work because Lennox Broster was working on people with 'disorders of sexual development' at Charing Cross during the 1930s and 1940s. Broster never operated on transsexuals and transvestites, being opposed to 'sex-change' surgery.[11] Initially Randell shared this view. In 1959

Randell wrote an article about fifty cases of transvestism and transsexualism seen by him. He completed an MD thesis at the University of Wales on the subject in 1960, discussing 61 male and 16 female patients. According to himself he saw an average of fifty new cases a year in the 1960s. In 1971 he gave a paper at a conference where he said that in 1969 44 males and 8 females had undergone surgery.[12]

Sometime during the 1960s (it is not officially recorded when exactly) surgeons linked to Charing Cross Hospital Gender Identity Clinic started to perform 'sex-change' surgery upon a minority of patients seen by John Randell. The timing of the advent of such surgery to the United Kingdom was significant. The sexual revolution and its ethos of turning conventional society upside down was the key contextual factor. Below I shall return to this in relation to family life and sexual attitudes. There were at the time numerous psychotherapists and psychiatrists who preferred a psychological approach and who were opposed to surgery and cross-sex hormone treatment. Following the lead of Harry Benjamin those in favour of surgery, who were driving the agenda for treatment, disregarded the new evidence for post-operative misery and failure, such as that of the wealthy American female-to-male transsexual Reed Erickson.[13] This is important because amid the current talk of regret and detransitioners, readers must understand that for as long as there have been 'sex-change operations' performed, there have been people who regretted undergoing them. Not only that but the Reed Erickson Foundation continued to promote the matter. It organised the first International Symposium on the subject in 1969.[14]

Then in the 1970s the annual number of patients seen by Randell increased from 100 to 200. This sounds very much like social contagion caused by increased media exposure during the sexual revolution. He claimed that around 30 patients a year underwent surgery during the 1970s. Randell reported that by 1980 he had seen 2438 patients, 1768 male and 670 female.[15] Randell worked alone for many years. In the late 1970s he acquired a clinical assistant, Dr. Guercken. The urologist who performed the surgery, Peter Philip, worked with him from the 1950s onwards. Precise figures for the number of people who underwent surgery during Randell's time at Charing Cross are not available though estimates are possible.[16]

Transsexual rights campaigning: 1960s – 1980s

The earliest groups in the United Kingdom for people now known as 'transgender', namely transvestites and transsexuals, were formed as chapters of American organisations. The American male transvestite Charles 'Virginia' Prince founded the Foundation for Personality Expression for male transvestites in 1960. In 1964 three British transvestites formed a British chapter, which became the Beaumont Society in 1966.[17] Most of the members were heterosexual male transvestites, apparently many married. Campaigning for specific rights for transsexuals began in the USA during the sexual revolution of the 1960s, and was at the heart of the counter-culture especially in cities such as San Francisco and New York City. Strategic litigation by transsexual rights activists for the legal right to amend sex on civil documents started in the late 1960s in New York State. The Supreme Court of New York State refused the modification of a transsexual's birth certificate in 1966, and defined sex chromosomally.[18] However in 1968 a tribunal in New York allowed for the first time modification of civil documents.[19]

Regarding the formation of groups in the UK, the Beaumont Society organised a conference in Leeds in 1974 to which a hundred people came along. A small British chapter of the Transexual Action Organisation (TAO) was formed in 1977. Stephen Whittle, a female-to-male transsexual who became a lawyer to fight for transsexual rights, claims to have started the Self Help Association for Transexuals (SHAFT), which became the Gender Trust.[20]

Soon western European transsexuals were taking cases to court, aiming at the European Court of Human Rights. The European Parliament initiated the move towards transsexual rights in law across EU member states with a resolution against discrimination against transsexuals on 12 September 1989, calling on the Council of Europe to enact a convention for the protection of transsexuals. On 29 September 1989 the Parliamentary Assembly of the Council of Europe adopted Recommendation 1117 proposed by the Italian Communist MEP Stefano Rodotà.[21]

Condition of transsexuals
Author(s): Parliamentary Assembly

Origin – Assembly debate on 29 September 1989 (21st Sitting) (see Doc. 6100, report of the Legal Affairs Committee, Rapporteur: Mr Rodotà). Text adopted by the Assembly on 29 September 1989 (21st Sitting).

The Assembly,

1. Considering that transsexualism is a syndrome characterised by a dual personality, one physical, the other psychological, together with such a profound conviction of belonging to the other sex that the transsexual person is prompted to ask for the corresponding bodily "correction" to be made;

2. Considering that modern medical progress, and in particular recourse to sexual conversion surgery, enable

transsexuals to be given the appearance and, to a great extent, the characteristics of the sex opposite to that which appears on their birth certificate;

3. Observing that this treatment is of a nature to bring the physical sex and the psychological sex into harmony with one another, and so give such persons a sexual identity which, moreover, constitutes a decisive feature of their personality

4. Believing that account of the changes brought about should be taken in the transsexual's civil status records by adding such details to the original record so as to update the data concerning sex in the birth certificate and identity papers, and by authorising a subsequent change of forename;

5. Considering that a refusal of such amendment of the civil status papers exposes persons in this situation to the risk of being obliged to reveal to numerous people the reasons for the discrepancy between their physical appearance and legal status;

6. Noting that transsexualism raises relatively new and complex questions to which states are called upon to find answers compatible with respect for human rights;

7. Observing that, in the absence of specific rules, transsexuals are often the victims of discrimination and violation of their private life;

8. Considering, furthermore, that the legislation of many member states is seriously deficient in this area and does not permit transsexuals, particularly those who have undergone an operation, to have civil status amendments made to take account of their appearance, external morphology, psychology and social behaviour;

9. Considering the case-law of the European Commission and Court of Human Rights;

10. Referring to the resolution which the European

Parliament adopted on 12 September 1989, in which, among other things, it called on the Council of Europe to enact a convention for the protection of transsexuals, 11. Recommends that the Committee of Ministers draw up a recommendation inviting member states to introduce legislation whereby, in the case of irreversible transsexualism:

a. the reference to the sex of the person concerned is to be rectified in the register of births and in the identity papers;

b. a change of forename is to be authorised;

c. the person's private life is to be protected;

d. all discrimination in the enjoyment of fundamental rights and freedoms is prohibited in accordance with Article 14 of the European Convention on Human Rights.

As the concept of 'psychological sex', originally from the USA, came via the Legal Affairs Committee of the Parliamentary Assembly of the Council of Europe, which was responsible for picking the judges of the European Court of Human Rights, it was only a matter of time before this idea entered the court's jurisprudence, enabling transsexual activists to win victories against member states of the Council of Europe.

Transsexual rights campaigning in the 1990s and early 2000s

The campaign group Press For Change (PFC) was formed in 1992 by Stephen Whittle.[22] PFC focused on legal and lobbying activity. Out of PFC ten activists formed the Gender Identity Research and Education Society (GIRES) in October 1997, an organisation which became a charity in 1998.[23] GIRES are still very active today. In 1994 Lynn Jones, the Labour MP for Selly Oak in Birmingham, along with Jane Playdon, formed the Parliamentary Forum for Transsexualism. The occasion for this was concern about transsexual prisoners brought up by a constituent.[24] During this period transsexual rights activists targeted key public institutions to influence them. Press For Change and the Gender and Sexuality Alliance (which closed in 1998) were invited by the Home Office in 1996 to prepare a report as part of a proposed review of Prison Service Guidelines regarding transsexual prisoners. The Home Secretary at the time was Michael Howard. A male-to-female transsexual called Kate More wrote Guideline proposals in June 1996.[25] This document cited Bryan Tully's three-year longitudinal study of transsexuals at Charing Cross Hospital Gender Identity Clinic in the 1980s, which found that over half of the male-to-female patients and roughly one third of the female-to-male patients had criminal backgrounds.[26] Kate More was also responsible for arguing that rape crisis centres for women should allow male-to-female transsexuals in. More also supported male-to-female transsexual/transgender prostitutes.[27]

Transgender rights campaigning in the 2000s focused on campaigning for the Gender Recognition Bill to become law. This was a Bill tabled by the Blair government in response to the UK losing a case at the European Court of Human Rights.[28] Specifically, the Department for Constitutional Affairs (previously the Lord Chancellor's Department and now the Ministry of Justice) conducted a Final Regulatory Impact Assessment for the Bill in November 2004 just before it was tabled in the House of Lords, looking at the costs of not implementing the Bill. Consideration was only really given to the risk of continued litigation by transsexual right activists.[29] No consideration was given to the effects on families and children, single-sex spaces, services and facilities, women's prisons, educational institutions, the quality and consistency of official data, the funding and staffing of the NHS, the effect on psychiatry and mental health, or other relevant fields.

Prevalence of transsexualism across the United Kingdom

Estimates of the self-identified transgender population today vary. Historically the term 'transsexual' was used, and confined by government departments to people who had had surgery and changed their civil records. In 1974 Hoenig published estimates of prevalence for England and Wales based on the Manchester region.[30] These came to 3 per 100,000 males (1 in 34,000), and 0.93 per 100,000 females (1 in 108,000). They found that transsexuals were much less likely than the general population of both sexes to be married, and to be disproportionately found among social classes IV and V. Hoenig et al. also argued, reasonably enough, that the higher number of transsexuals in metropolitan areas would be due to male transsexuals being more ready to migrate to cities. Nothing has changed in this respect to either these findings.[31] Hoenig et al. calculated that at the time of writing there were 537 male and 187 female transsexuals in England and Wales. Evidence for Northern Ireland was published in 1981, showing an average of 2 patients per year were seen in Belfast.[32] Prevalence was estimated at 1 in 52,000. This 1981 study of transsexuals in Northern Ireland who had visited the hospital in Belfast for the previous fourteen years, i.e. since 1967, found that around half of patients only started experiencing difficulties on or after puberty. Thus the early evidence does not substantiate any claim that all transsexual/ transgender people are 'born that way'. The numbers in Northern Ireland have risen since then, but apart from 65 diagnoses in 2012/2013, with less than five being main diagnoses, there were none in subsequent years. Prevalence in Scotland was reported in 1999 on the basis of a large-scale survey of Scottish GPs at 8.18 per 100,000. Divided by sex, this came to 13.44 per 100,000 males and 3.21 per 100,000 females.[33] From this we see that prevalence in Scotland by 1999 was considerably higher especially for males than in England and Wales in 1974, or in Northern Ireland in 1981. The Scottish figures were cited several times by transsexual rights activists in the run-up to the Gender Recognition Act.

Accounting for different levels of prevalence historically and across countries

The prevalence of transsexualism has historically varied across countries. Papers on this subject have been written by staff at Gender Identity Clinics and similar institutions, and as such it is significant they have not delved very deeply into possible reasons. In reality, clinicians writing on the prevalence of transsexualism are similar to many social scientists – more or less socially liberal in their presuppositions and prejudices. There is thus an in-built bias towards assuming higher prevalence rates are the norm for all populations. This is based on the myth that transsexualism is a given in human nature, even though there is no evidence that it is genetic.[34] It is also based on the myth that lots of people are hiding their transsexualism for fear of societal prejudice, and moreover on the moralising position that they should not be hiding this from others. In reality, not only does prevalence vary over time but so do sex-ratios. In Poland a conservative Catholic country, more transsexuals were born female than male.[35] It is reasonable to suggest that in a more traditional society females will be more likely to see the social life and perceived status of males as enviable, whereas in a more socially liberal society, males will be more likely to see the social life and perceived status of females as enviable.

Prevalence rates by country over time[36]

Sweden (1967) – 1 in 37,000 males; 1 in 103,000 females

USA (1968) 1 in 100,000 males; 1:400,000 females

Germany (former Federal Republic) (1993) 1 in 42,000 males; 1 in 104,000 females

Poland (1988) – 5.5: 1 female/male sex at birth ratio

Netherlands (1980) – 1 in 45,000 males; 1 in 200,000 females

Netherlands (1990) – 1 in 11,900 males, and 1 in 30,400 females

France (2000) – 1 in 100,000

Belgium (2007) – 1 in 12,900 males; 1 in 33,800 females

Prevalence was lower in Wallonia, the French-speaking part of Belgium, than in Flanders, the Dutch-speaking part. The authors of the cited study said this was due to less acceptance of transsexualism in Wallonia, but did not inquire why this might be. A closer inspection of the literature on transsexualism as well as cultural differences furnishes a reason. French speakers have always seen transsexualism as an American phenomenon.[37] This attitude would likely be found in the French-speaking part of Belgium. The Flemish-speaking part, on the other hand, would likely have been influenced by the more liberal approach in the Netherlands, where more people speak fluent English. It has also been estimated to be very low in Italy, which is probably the most socially conservative country in western Europe, traditionally with the highest rate of churchgoing. Italy belies the complaint of LGB opponents of transgender ideology, who see in it a version of traditional conservative values.[38]

There are numerous possible explanations for the rise in incidence of diagnosis. Put simply, over the last fifty years more people have come to consider themselves as having a gender identity disorder, mainly transsexualism. The available evidence has long shown that such people have a lower than average rate of marriage and childbearing.[39] However, contrary to what numerous people have said over the years, transgender self-identification is not simply a cover for same-sex orientation. Today LGB and feminist critics of gender reassignment argue that it is motivated by homophobia and that it is 'conversion therapy by any other name'. This is ironic given that the concept of 'a female soul trapped in a male body' was invented by Karl Ulrichs, a German homosexual rights lawyer who used it to make sense of his own homosexuality in the 1860s.[40] Recent surveys suggest that around half are heterosexual or bisexual and a small but significant minority are asexual; indeed transgender people seem more likely to be asexual or to lack sexual experience than the general population.[41] What we have here, arguably, is an increase in people with a sense of failed sexual identity on the one hand and on the other who are inevitably part of a hedonistic society where celibacy is socially unacceptable. It is worth asking whether some people are identifying themselves as transgender because they have little sexual interest in the opposite sex yet know that they are not attracted to the same sex. For some individuals, it is worth asking whether a sense of social and personal failure due to this contributed to the development of a wish to escape by identifying as a member of the opposite sex. This could be the case in our contemporary western culture which heavily stigmatises celibacy for various reasons.[42] Such questions do not get asked in a secular or anti-Christian cultural climate, yet they need to be asked because the rise of transsexualism came historically with the intensification of secularisation and the move to permissiveness and hedonism in the sphere of sexuality and the self. Hoenig and colleagues found that female-to-male transsexuals were disproportionately likely to be only children. This is interesting because cross-cultural research has found that all over the world parents tend to have a sexist bias in favour of having a son as the first-born child, thus mirroring those studies which find that male-to-female transsexuals were more likely to be sons of mothers who wanted daughters having already had sons.[43] From a wider perspective the rise in the prevalence of transsexualism is not surprising given that such a self-concept as transsexualism has increased with the inward, subjective turn of modernity, itself accompanied by a drop in birth-rates. Again these are all facets of long-term secularisation.[44]

These international differences in prevalence do not tell us anything about the prevalence of gender incongruence, i.e. discomfort with belonging to one's sex which does not extent as far as a desire to live permanently as a member of the opposite sex, in any country. Unfortunately there appear to be no statistics available on this. Thus we cannot measure whether in some countries people who experience such discomfort are more likely to label themselves transsexuals or to be diagnosed as such by psychiatrists. In addition, clinicians looking at prevalence have not delved into the possible link to other demographic factors such as population density. Prevalence turns out to be higher in countries with higher population density, such as England and the Netherlands. Social contact and networking play a part in greater prevalence of transsexualism, seeing as it is spread partly by suggestion and social contact. It would be worth researching the extent to which the rise of transgender internet sites and social media pages have levelled out the differences between countries and regions, especially among children and adolescents.

Transsexualism and the field of mental health
In the United Kingdom transsexualism has from the beginning been treated within mental health and subsequently

through endocrinology and plastic surgery. A major challenge in the field is whether a patient's transsexualism is primary or secondary, i.e. the main disorder or an epiphenomenon of an existing psychiatric disorder. It is well-established that transsexuals may also have other psychiatric disorders, such as schizophrenia, bipolar disorder, depression, Obsessive-Compulsive Disorder, anxiety, Body Dysmorphic Disorder, and various Personality Disorders.[45] The more rigorous mental health professionals realise the need to assess all patients who initially present themselves as suffering from gender dysphoria to see whether gender discomfort is not in reality an aspect of one or more of these.

Treatment protocols for transsexualism, now known as 'gender dysphoria', vary across the United Kingdom. In England, Scotland and Northern Ireland any patient who goes to their GP stating that they consider themselves to suffer from gender dysphoria can be referred straightaway to a Gender Identity Clinic. This means that most patients in the UK are allowed to bypass initial psychiatric assessment. NHS Wales requires all patients to be referred by their GP to the psychiatric team of their local health board for initial assessment to see whether they have another psychiatric condition.[46] The situation elsewhere in the UK can only be because of successful infiltration – entryism by transgender activists, who have been allowed to rewrite the rules and protocols for treatment on their own terms. In addition there seem to be more and more psychologists and psychotherapists, and fewer psychiatrists involved. This is a problem because it is psychiatrists who are permitted to make a diagnosis of a mental health condition. In reality non-medically trained mental health professionals are probably involved precisely because gender dysphoria is no longer officially considered to be a psychiatric disorder. The problem then is that if patients are initially referred to them, they may well be less likely to realise that a patient needs assessment by a qualified psychiatrist. All this raises the question of why gender reassignment treatment should be funded by the NHS, which is a healthcare system geared towards treating the sick, and paid for by taxpayers even if those never use the NHS.

Effect on family life

Transsexualism has often had a detrimental effect on family life. We have already seen that evidence from the Charing Cross Hospital Gender Identity Clinic in the 1980s indicated that a substantial minority of male and female patients were married, and a number of these had children. Over the years the press has reported on quite a few cases of women divorcing male transsexuals due to the distress their determination to seek out 'sex-change' treatment caused them and their children. Christian families have not been insulated from these problems. At the 1998 conference of GENDYS (a 'network for transgendered people'), Diana Aitchison from Women of the Beaumont Society (WOBS), the sister organisation of the Beaumont Society, talked of how around 100 women a year end up in psychiatric wards due to the negative effects of their husband's cross-dressing and fantasies about being 'a woman'.[47] The WOBS pages started carrying this claim in November 2002. Thus it is possible to infer that the estimate of 100 women a year in the UK ending up in psychiatric wards comes from knowledge gained by WOBS as a support group. There is no officially available data on the number of males who underwent gender reassignment before 1998. However in 2000 the UK government published a Report of the Interdepartmental Working Group on Transsexual People, which estimated the number of male-to-female transsexuals as between 1300 and 2000. As gender reassignment had been practised since the late 1960s, if 100 wives a year were crying out for help because of 100 husbands, over 30 years this would come to 3000 couples. In reality the number was probably lower as referral rates were much higher in the 1990s than previously. In the mid-1980s it was found that around nearly half of male patients at Charing Cross had been married. If this percentage held good for the period before 2000, then it is reasonable to suppose that most wives and partners had been adversely affected. Interestingly the WOBS article remained on their website until September 2012, so long after the passing of the Gender Recognition Act. Clearly WOBS considered it important to keep on telling the truth to women looking for help. In light of this, it is highly significant that hardly any academic literature exists on the families of transsexuals and on the effect of transsexualism on other family members, notably spouses and children where the person diagnosed is married. This is no accident. History clearly shows that the doctors supporting surgical and hormonal treatment all had sexually libertarian attitudes.[49]

In this context it is worth considering the papers of Richard Green, formerly consultant psychiatrist at Charing Cross Hospital Gender Identity Clinic, who started his career in the USA working with John Money, and who went on to produce influential studies on boys diagnosed with Gender Identity Disorder. Green wrote several times on the children of transsexuals, claiming they hardly suffered disturbance due to their fathers' transsexualism. However, he did not have a random sample but only a very small handpicked number of cases.[50] This is curious because by the late 1980s there would have been quite a number of men who had fathered children passing through the Gender Identity Clinic. That said, I have been told by West London Mental Health Trust that indicating one's marital status was optional, thus it could be that some patients chose not to disclose it.[51] Other

Gender Clinic staff have written on children of transsexuals. They found that between 1989 and March 2001, 32 out of 196 children and adolescents referred to the Gender Identity Development Service in London were children of a transsexual parent. The clinicians studied data about 18 children of transsexuals, ten girls and eight boys. They seemed pleased that only one of the girls had symptoms of Gender Identity Disorder, and on this basis dismissed worries that the identity of children of transsexuals could be damaged by the parents undergoing gender reassignment. However, if for the sake of argument this is taken to be a representative sample, this means 1/18 children of transsexuals develop Gender Identity Disorder before reaching adulthood. That's 5.56%, which is far higher than the percentage of children in the general population who do. The clinicians also found that children of transsexuals were less likely than other children and adolescents who had been referred to be suffering from depression, and this again was used as evidence for the children not being adversely affected. They should have made the connection with their own evidence that most of these children were no longer living with the (mostly male) transsexual parents, but with (mostly female) non-transsexual parents and their new partners and children. It is reasonable to suppose that this move away from an atmosphere where transsexualism dominated family dynamics would have led to improved mental health and protected them against depression and, given staff's professional investment in the 'system' which permits surgical and hormonal treatments and thus in allowing a parent to 'change gender', we have to ask whether children in these cases had not in fact 'frozen' psychologically and worn a mask to protect themselves from trauma.[52]

We have to wonder whether family members who are unhappy with a relative's 'sex-change' have not approached

Gender Clinics for psychological help as they might perceive the Gender Clinics as being guilty of colluding with their relatives' fantasies. Anecdotally I am unaware of any of the numerous family members who were unhappy with their relative's gender reassignment who have approached Gender Identity Clinics for help for themselves. Indeed the whole idea of giving psychological 'help' to relatives has long been pushed by transsexual/transgender activists as a means of trying to manipulate relatives into accepting their chosen sex/gender and coercing them into using the person's new opposite-sex/gender name and pronouns. This is an attempt at enforced lying and is highly abusive.

Given the fact of family breakup, transgender rights activists have of course tried to steer the family courts in their own direction. Even since the passing of the Gender Recognition Act the courts have stood up to activists' unrealistic and often harmful demands. These cases have not always had the publicity they deserve from the press. There are some very important judgments from the Family Courts that have been published recently. The first was in December 2015 with Her Honour Judge Moir presiding at Newcastle Crown Court. The second was in 2016 with Mr Justice Hayden presiding at the Family Division of the High Court in London.[53] Both cases involved boys who had been deliberately cross-dressed and brought up as girls by their mothers, neither of whom wanted a boy. In the first case other relatives also joined in, and the mother even suggested to her son he might have a 'sex-change operation' when he was older, like a transgender colleague of hers whom she introduced to him. In both cases the judges awarded the boys to the custody of other relatives, the grandparents and the father. In the second case the judge expressed the view that there are children who are 'truly transgender' and that these should be treated as such. No such opinion was proffered in the first. Despite the judge in the first case permitting publication of the judgment, the press did not report the case. The fact that the first case was not reported in the press whereas the second was is evidence of press bias against fundamental disagreement with the whole notion of being 'truly' transgender, i.e. 'truly born in the wrong body'. Such bias can only have come about due to non-discrimination codes reliant on gender reassignment being a protected characteristic under the Equality Act 2010, itself building on the Gender Recognition Act.

In 2002 the NHS still recognised that some children develop gender dysphoria because their parents cross-dressed them as children, and that because the parents were disappointed that the child was not of the sex they wanted. By now the NHS does not recognise this problem at all.[54] It is fully signed-up to the doctrine that children are 'born that way', *something most British people do not believe*. We know this from a survey that the press did not bother to report in October 2016, undoubtedly because it contradicted LGBT propaganda. The International Lesbian, Gay, Bisexual, Transgender and Intersex Association (ILGA) conducted the largest ever global survey of attitudes towards LGBTI people, and published the findings in two instalments, in May and October 2016.[55]

'Do you believe that people who do not identify with the sex they were assigned at birth...?'
Are born that way – 30%; Become so – 13%; Chose to be so – 18%; Don't know – 39%

Thus even though the UK has been a European and world leader in transgender ideology and rights, most of the public simply do not believe the notion of people being born transgender, which is essentially what the transgender movement has long claimed in the law courts by saying that people have a 'psychological sex'.

Regret, reversing gender reassignment and return to live as a member of one's sex

From time to time clinical researchers have estimated rates of regret of gender reassignment surgery among patients. There are problems with this research.[56] The most obvious problem is that it is conducted by people connected to gender identity clinics, who may be perceived as having a vested interest in perpetuating and promoting the gender identity clinic system and ethos. Thus patients may well be telling them what they sense is socially acceptable. The fact that professionals from within the world of gender identity clinics have been starting to speak out in favour of detransitioners, even saying that there is a stigma around detransition, is important.[57] There are no official statistics on how many people change back to living as a member of their sex. Nevertheless, I believe it is possible to identify instances within Hospital Episode Statistics for NHS England and the Patient Episode Database for Wales for NHS Wales because operations are listed as 'male-to-female' and 'female-to-male' as well as for 'male' and 'female' people. As the NHS lists gender reassignment (or as it is called, 'sexual transformation surgery') under the phenotypic sex of the patients (sex as determined by appearance and endocrinology, not genotypic sex, which is determined by chromosomes), people born male who undergo surgery to appear female are listed as females, and vice versa. However this must mean that if a person listed as female is said to have undergone female-to-male sexual transformation surgery, this must be a case of a male-to-female transsexual who appeared female but underwent reverse surgery. The numbers for such surgery have been very small so far, just under one or two a year, as it is not routinely commissioned on the NHS. There is also anecdotal evidence from the press and social media that there are people who change back, though some of these would be people who had been taking cross-sex hormones but had not undergone genital surgery. The world of Gender Identity Clinics knows about this and has confirmed this in response to several Freedom of Information Requests. They have also promised for several years to publish datasets based on this information, but have yet to do so.[58]

Conclusion

The transgender war on the mind and mental health

Transsexual/transgender rights activists have always opposed psychological treatment for gender dysphoria as either impossible or offensive (to them). Harry Benjamin, who was not psychiatrically trained, was particularly strident in this respect. Speaking of the USA, the American therapist Leslie Lothstein, who specialised in the treatment of female-to-male transsexualism and who pioneered the psychotherapeutic treatment of transsexualism, said forty years ago that 'the pervasive anti-psychiatry tradition among transsexual clinicians made it all but impossible for transsexuals to be referred to psychotherapy prior to 1970'.[59] The question that nobody is asking in the debates over treatment is: why have psychological treatments been increasingly stigmatised, especially here in the United Kingdom? I believe we need to look at the enthroning of the concept of 'gender identity' and the absence of the concept of the mind in the field, for it is the mind which is the core concept of psychiatry and psychology. Without it patients have no higher reference than their own fleeting self-image and thoughts, and become prisoners of madness. The mind is something that is inferred from our experience as well as posited *a priori* by the major religions and philosophies, as is the soul. The mental health professions are silent on this, and do not discuss the possibility that the stigma attached to mental illness is exacerbated by the materialist view of the human person which is the result of secularisation and atheism. Not only that, but gender ideologues posit a plurality of gender identities which, given that they are inventions, exhibit an infinity of possibilities, including a person having more than one at the same time. If the ideology of Gender Identity could speak, it might well say 'My name is Legion, for we are many.'

Notes

[1] I am indebted for the history recounted here to Joanne Meyerowitz, *How Sex Changed: A History of Transsexuality in the United States*. Cambridge, Mass.: Harvard University Press, 2004: 15-50.

[2] Scientists had discovered hormones in the late 19th century and acknowledged chromosomes as the more fundamental determinants of sex in the early 20th century. Debates on the biological definition of sex were started by advocates of 'sex-change' surgery and cross-sex hormone treatment who wanted to make hormones, not chromosomes, the basis of this. Meyerowitz, *How Sex Changed*, 27.

[3] Meyerowitz, *How Sex Changed*, 112.

[4] Meyerowitz, *How Sex Changed*, 114ff.

[5] John Colapinto, *As Nature Made Him: The Boy Who Was Raised as a Girl*. New York: Harper, 1997.

[6] Judith Reisman unmasked Alfred Kinsey as an intellectual fraud who was morally bankrupt in Judith A. Reisman and Edward W. Eichel, *Kinsey, Sex and Fraud: The Indoctrination of a People*. Lafayette, Louisiana: Lochinvar Inc., 1990. See also her website http://www.drjudithreisman.com/the_kinsey_coverup.html

[7] Meyerowitz, *How Sex Changed*, 48. Katherine M. Ramsland, *Inside the Mind of Healthcare Serial Killers: Why They Kill*. Greenwood Publishing, 2007: 25.

[8] Sue Surkes, 'Honeytraps and birthday calls: Secret file reveals Mossad efforts to net Mengele', *The Times of Israel*, 5 September 2017. https://www.timesofisrael.com/honeytraps-and-birthday-calls-secret-file-reveals-

mossad-efforts-to-net-mengele/

[9] By now most people familiar with social media trends will be aware of the ongoing attacks by male-born transgender activists against secular women seeking to defend single-sex spaces and facilities for females.

[10] Randall's biography from the Royal College of Physicians can be read at http://munksroll.rcplondon.ac.uk/Biography/Details/3696

[11] Obituary for Lennox Broster, *British Medical Journal* 1, 1965: 1130.

[12] John Bulmer Randell, *Cross-dressing and the desire to change sex*. M.D. Thesis. Cardiff: Welsh National School of Medicine, University of Wales, Cardiff, 1960. For the figures quoted, see Dave King and Richard Ekins, 'Pioneers of Transgendering: John Randell, 1918-1982', Gendys 2002, the Seventh International Gender Dysphoria Conference, Manchester, England, 2002. http://www.gender.org.uk/conf/2002/king22.htm

[13] Harry Benjamin, 'Transvestism and Transsexualism', *International Journal of Sexology* 7, 1953, 12-14. Benjamin attacked all psychotherapy in relation to transsexualism and transvestism.

[14] The First International Symposium on Gender Dysphoria was held at the Piccadilly Hotel in London, 25-27 July 1969, and co-sponsored by the Erickson Educational Foundation and the Albany Trust, a gay rights group. The chair was Prof. C. J. Dewhurst of Queen Charlotte's Hospital, London. One of the speakers was Labour MP David Kerr, Vice-President of the Socialist Medical Association, which was and is affiliated to the Labour Party. http://www.wpath.org/site_page.cfm?pk_association_webpage_menu=1347&pk_association_webpage=4229

[15] http://www.gender.org.uk/conf/2002/king22.htm

[16] GIRES estimated in 2008 that only around 10, 000 had hitherto presented themselves for treatment for gender dysphoria. This is a credible estimate given the rise in referrals since 1999 when local NHS boards were legally required not to refuse gender reassignment. Yet GIRES also claimed, without providing supporting evidence, that 'the adults who present emerge from a large reservoir of transgender people, who experience some degree of gender variance. They may number 300,000, a prevalence of 600 per 100,000, of whom 80% were assigned boys at birth. However, the number would be nearly 500, 000, if the gender balance among transgender people is equal.' Bernard Reed, Stephenne Rhodes, Dr. Pietà Schofield, Professor Kevan Wylie, *Gender Variance in the UK: Prevalence, Incidence, Growth and Geographic Distribution*, GIRES, 2009: 4. https://web.archive.org/web/20100215040008/http://gires.org.uk:80/assets/Medpro-Assets/GenderVarianceUK-report.pdf Curiously the article is no longer up on the GIRES website.

[17] Mel Porter, 'Gender identity and sexual orientation', in Pat Thane (ed.), *Unequal Britain: Equalities in Britain since 1945*. London: Bloomsbury, 2010: 147-148.

[18] Anonymous vs. Weiner: 270, New York States, 2d, 319. Source, PHC p. 482. Joanne Meyerowitz, *How sex changed: A history of transsexuality in the United States*. Cambridge, Mass.: Harvard University Press, 2004: 242-245.

[19] *In re* Anonymous, 293, New York State, pp. 834-838, 1968. Source, PHC, p. 483

[20] This evidence is from the TRANS-ACADEMIC archives on JISCM@ ail, 1 June 1999. https://www.jiscmail.ac.uk/cgi-bin/webadmin?A2=trans-academic;d79f3aba.99 Also see http://www.lawsociety.org.uk/Policy-campaigns/documents/Stephen-Whittle-bio-June-2015/

[21] http://assembly.coe.int/nw/xml/XRef/Xref-XML2HTML-en. asp?fileid=15151&lang=en

[22] Press For Change, http://www.pfc.org.uk

[23] GIRES, http://www.gires.org.uk

[24] http://www.lynnejones.org.uk/lynne-jones-mp/transsex.htm#forum

[25] https://web.archive.org/web/19990506043352/http://www.pfc.org. uk:80/legal/tsprison.htm

[26] Bryan Tully, *Accounting for Transsexualism and Transhomosexuality*. London: Whiting and Birch Ltd, 1992: 267.

[27] Kate More and Sandra Laframboise with Deborah Brady, 'Testimonies of HIV Activism', in Stephen Whittle and Kate More (eds.), *Reclaiming Genders: Transsexual Grammars at the Fin de Siecle*. London: Bloomsbury [1999], 2016: 144. http://www.gender.org.uk/gendys/bookshop/more.htm

[28] The decision of the European Court of Human Rights in the case of Goodwin v. United Kingdom in 2002 gave transsexuals the right to change the sex/gender on their birth certificates. https://hudoc.echr.coe. int/eng#%7B22itemid%22001-60596%22%5D%7D

[29] The Final Regulatory Impact Assessment for the Gender Recognition Bill was published in November 2003, with three Options. Option 1 was 'Do nothing': 'The government is obliged to breaches of international law. A declaration of incompatibility with the [European] Convention [of Human Rights] can be made by a UK court and its effect is similar, i.e. if the government does nothing, the pressure to legislate will continue to build and further challenges and claims for compensation will continue to be brought.' The other options were a remedial order or primary legislation. http://webarchive.nationalarchives.gov.uk/20040722074350/http://www.dca.gov.uk/risl/grbria.htm

[30] J. Hoenig and J. C. Kenna, 'The Prevalence of Transsexualism in England and Wales', *British Journal of Psychiatry* 124, 1974, 181-190.

[31] In the mid-1980s Tully found the same picture obtained, see Tully, *Accounting for Transsexualism*, Appendix 2, 261-269.

[32] Ethna C. O'Gorman, 'A Preliminary Report on Transsexualism in

Northern Ireland', *Ulster Medical Journal* 50, 1981, 46-49.

[33] Philip Wilson, Clare Sharp and Susan Carr, 'The prevalence of gender dysphoria in Scotland: a primary care study', *British Journal of General Practice,* December 1999: 991-992.

[34] The relevant studies are studies on monozygotic twins or studies finding that male-to-female transsexuals, like homosexuals, are more likely to have older brothers. These are summarised in Kenneth J. Zucker and Susan J. Bradley, *Gender Identity Disorder and Psychosexual Problems in Children and Adolescents.* New York: The Guilford Press, 1995: 127-129. It is significant that both the incidence and prevalence of transsexualism appears to have increased at the same time as the birth-rate has declined below replacement level across most western countries. This would seem to rule out a genetic cause.

[35] Julian Godlewski, 'Transsexualism and anatomic sex ratio reversal in Poland', *Archives of Sexual Behavior* 17(6), December 1988: 547-548.

[36] Sweden (1967): Jan Wålinder, 'Transsexualism: Definition, Prevalence and Sex Distribution'; M. Landén, J. Wålindel, B. Lundström, 'Incidence and sex ratio of transsexualism in Sweden', *Acta Psychiatrica Scandinavica* 93(4) April 1996: 261-263; Stig-Eric Olsson and Anders R. Möller, 'On the Incidence and Sex Ratio of Trnassexualims in Sweden, 1972-2002', *Archives of Sexual Behavior* 32(4) August 2003: 381-386; Ira Pauly, 'The current status of change of sex operation', *Journal of Nervous and Mental Diseases* 147(1968) 460-471; L. Garrels, G. Kockott, N. Michael, W. Preuss, K. Renter, G. Schmidt, V. Sigusch, K. Windgassen, 'Sex ratio of transsexuals in Germany: the development over three decades', *Acta Psychiatrica Scandinavica* 102(6) December 2000: 445-448; Netherlands (1980): P.L.E. Eklund, L. J. G. Gooren and P. D. Bezemer, 'Prevalence of Transsexualism in the Netherlands', *British Journal of Psychiatry* 152(1988)638-640; Netherlands (1990): A. Bakker, P. J. M. Van Kesteren, L. J. G. Gooren and P. D. Bezemer, 'The Prevalence of transsexualism in the Netherlands', *Acta Psychiatrica Scandinavica* 87(4) April 1993: 237-238; Belgium (2007): G. De Cuypere, M. Van Hemelrijck, A. Michel, B. Carael, G. Heylens, R. Rubens, P. Hoebeke, S. Monstrey, 'Prevalence and demography of transsexualism in Belgium', *European Psychiatry* 22(3) April 2007: 137-141.

[37] André Plichet, 'Le désir de changer de sexe, forme épidémique d'un mal ancien', *Presse médicale* 64(41) 1956: 949-951. The very notion of 'gender-neutral language' could only ever have been dreamt up by people who only speak English, as French like most European languages is grammatically gendered.

[38] In the context of current debates on allowing male-to-female transgender offenders into women's prisons, it is worth noting that Italy has a designated prison for transgender offenders, thus managing to solve the

problem of safety on both sides. Pat Eggleton, 'Italy to open world's first prison for transgender inmates', 14 January 2010, *Italy Magazine* http://www.italymagazine.com/italy/firenze-province/italy-open-worlds-first-prison-transgender-inmates

[39] Tully found that 11 out of 34 MtF patients who achieved surgery had been married, whereas 55 out of 109 MtF patients who did not had been married. For FtM patients the figures were 3 out of 26 and 2 out of 35. Tully, *Accounting for Transsexualism*, 263.

[40] Karl Heinrich Ulrichs, *The Riddle of "Man-Manly" Love: The Pioneering Work on Male Homosexuality*. Vol. 1. Buffalo: Prometheus, 1994: 58.

[41] Scottish Transgender Alliance, NHS England

[42] Elizabeth Abbott, *A History of Celibacy*. Cambridge, Mass: Da Capo Press, 2001. There is some research suggesting that students who do not desire sexual activity are viewed negatively by heterosexuals. Cara C. MacInnis and Gordon Hodson, 'Integroup bias toward "Group X": Evidence of prejudice, dehumanizaiton, avoidance, and discrimination against asexuals', *Group Processes and Intergroup Relations*, 2012: 2-12.

[43] Hoenig et al. N. E. Wiliamson, *Sons or Daughters: A cross-cultural survey of parental preferences*. Beverley Hills, CA: Sage, 1976.

[44] Charles Taylor, *Sources of the Self: The Making of Modern Identity*. Cambridge: Cambridge University Press, 1989. William Sims Bainbridge relates demographic research on fertility to theories of secularization in 'Fertility and Secularization' in Bron Taylor (ed.), *Encyclopedia of Religion and Nature*. London: A & C Black, 2008: 656-658.

[45] In the Netherlands in 2003, psychiatrists were surveyed on this question. They reported on 584 patients with 'cross-gender identification', finding that in only 225 (39%) of cases was Gender Identity Disorder (aka transsexualism) the primary diagnosis. See Joost à Campo, Henk Nijman, H. Merckelbach and Catharine Evers, 'Psychiatric Comorbidity of Gender Identity Disorders: A Survey Among Dutch Psychiatrists', *American Journal of Psychiatry* 160(7), July 2003: 1332-1336. Research on comorbidity has continued in the Netherlands since then. See U. Hepp, B. Kraemer, U. Schnyder, N. Miller and A. Delsignore, 'Psychiatric comorbidity in gender identity disorder', *Journal of Psychosomatic Research* 48(3) March 2005: 259-261. In this study most patients fulfilled the criteria for Axis I disorders, and 42% of the patients were diagnosed with one or more personality disorders. On schizophrenia and transsexualism, see P. Scherrer & J. C. Pelletier, 'From transsexualism to schizophrenia', *Annales Médico-Psychologiques*, 2(5), 1972: 609-635. Charles David Mellon, Carrolee Barlow, Joshua Cook and Lincoln D. Clark, 'Autocastration and autopenectomy in a patient with transsexualism and schizophrenia', *The Journal of Sex Research* 26(1) 1989: 125-130.

It is instructive to note individual cases where schizophrenic patients who then developed transsexualism were subsequently cured of both disorders through drugs. See Rameez Zafar, 'Schizophrenia and gender identity disorder', *British Journal of Psychiatry* 32(8), July 2008: On Obsessive-Compulsive Disorder and transsexualism, see Isaac Marks, Richard Green and David Mataix-Cols, 'Adult gender identity disorder can remit', *Comprehensive Psychiatry* 41(4), July 2000: 273-275. On Bipolar Disorder and transsexualism, see E. Habermeyer, I. Kamps and W. Kawohl, 'A Case of Bipolar Psychosis and Transsexualism', *Psychopathology* 36, 2003: 168-70. A study conducted in the USA in 2003 found transsexuals to have similar levels of Dissociative Experiences as other psychiatric inpatients, with both being higher than the normal population. The reason for the higher score among transsexuals than the normal population was due to traumatic childhood experiences. Annette Kersting, Michael Reutemann, Ursual Gast, Patricia Ohrmann, Thomas Suslow, Nikolaus Michael and Volker Arolt, 'Dissociative Disorders and Traumatic Childhood Experiences in Transsexuals', *Journal of Nervous and Mental Diseases*, 191(3), March 2003: 182-189. Transsexuals of both sexes have been found to be at higher risk of eating disorders as well. See Silja Vocks, Catharina Stahn, Kerstin Loenser and Tanja Legenbauer, 'Eating and Body Image Disturbances in Male-to-Female and Female-to-Male Transsexuals', *Archives of Sexual Behaviour* 38(3), June 2009: 364-377.

[46] http://www.gmc-uk.org/guidance/ethical_guidance/28852.asp

[47] http://www.gender.org.uk/conf/1998/diana.htm

[48] *Report of the Interdepartmental Working Group on Transsexual People.* London: Home Office, 2000: 3
http://webarchive.nationalarchives.gov.uk/20020802071051/http://www.lcd.gov.uk:80/constitution/transsex/transpeo.htm
In 1992 Bryan Tully found out that 66 out of 143 male patients (46%) had been married, and that 48 (34%) had children. Eleven of those who had been married and six of those who had children underwent surgery. Bryan Tully, *Accounting for Transsexualism and Transhomosexuality.* London: Whiting & Birch, 1992: 263-264.

[49] Meyerowitz, *How Sex Changed*, 217.

[50] Richard Green, 'Transsexuals' Children', *International Journal of Transgenderism* 2(4) December 1998. http://www.symposium.com/ijt/ijtc0601.htm

[51] Personal email communication in response to Freedom of Information Request.

[52] David Freedmand, Fiona Tasker and Domenico Di Ceglie, 'Children and Adolescents with Transsexual Parents Referred to a Specialist Gender Identity Development Service: A Brief Report of Key Developmental

Features', *Clinical Child Psychology and Psychiatry* July 2002. http://ccp.sagepub.com/cgi/content/abstract/7/3/423.

[53] G (A Child) [2015] EWFC B209; J(a minor) [2016] EWFC 2430

[54] http://web.archive.org/web/20020813193915/http://www.nhsdirect.nhs.uk:80/nhsdoheso/display.asp?sSection=Whyitisnecessary&sTopic=Genderreassignment

[55] http://ilga.org/what-we-do/ilga-riwi-global-attitudes-survey-lgbti-logo/; http://ilga.org/personal-political-attitudes-lgbti-survey/. The percentage of people in the UK who believe that people who do not identify with their sex, i.e. transgender people, were 'born that way', is lower than the percentage in the following countries: Ireland, Australia, New Zealand, Canada, Croatia, Serbia, Portugal, Spain, Netherlands, Italy, Chile, Israel.

[56] Colette Chiland gives a very precise criticism of this research in Colette Chiland, *Transsexualism: Illusion and Reality.* London: Continuum, 2003: 90-118.

[57] Dr. Miroslav Djordjevic, a Serbian surgeon, was interviewed on 1 October 2017 by the Telegraph, 'Sex change regret: Gender reversal surgery is on the rise, so why aren't we talking about it?'. http://www.telegraph.co.uk/health-fitness/body/gender-reversal-surgery-rise-arent-talking/

[58] For example, in 2010 Charing Cross Gender Identity Clinic, then the largest clinic in the UK, admitted that they saw 'a lot' of detransitioners, and were planning to research the phenomenon. They even claimed that Nottingham Gender Clinic, the second largest clinic in the UK, also saw a lot. https://www.whatdotheyknow.com/request/a_dishonest_foi_response_from_th. More recently, the Tavistock and Portman NHS Trust, who currently run the Gender Clinic in London and the GIDS for children and adolescents, said that they plan to publish their database on young people who cease to undergo physiological treatments and 'detransition'.https://tavistockandportman.nhs.uk/documents/771/FOI_17-18124_GIDS_Questionnaires_and_Treatment_Cessation.pdf and https://tavistockandportman.nhs.uk/documents/641/FOI_16-17254_Gender_Dysphoria_Treatment.pdf

[59] Leslie Lothstein, *Female-to-Male Transsexualism: Historical, Clinical and Theoretical Issues*, London: Routledge & Kegan Paul, 1983: 264.

5

'I'M TRANSGENDER': HOW TO RESPOND

Daniel Moody

Introduction

I have spent the past four years of my life immersed in all things 'gender': gender identity, gender expression, gender performativity; gender theory, gender ideology, gender mainstreaming; cisgender, transgender.... My approach is that of the philosopher, rather than that of the medical practitioner, theologian, researcher, or lawyer—although we will be discussing law quite a lot.

In terms of this book *The New Normal*, the question of how to respond to transgenderism is the question of how to respond to a huge and rapid political and cultural shift in our attitude towards the nature and meaning of human personhood. But, of course, we cannot know how to respond to something unless we first know what that something is. After all, we need to know why that thing warrants a response. Likewise, we cannot know how to respond to transgenderism without first knowing what gender is.

With that in mind, the subject will be broken down into three parts. Part one is 'What is gender?' What does that word mean and, just as importantly, what does it not mean? Part two addresses the way in which sex and gender relate to one another, and part three looks at some of the ways in which we can respond to this ideology.

Background Snapshot

Before we start, though, we need to make sure we are fully aware of the context in which we are having this discussion. So let us mention briefly four of the many ways in which the ideas of gender identity and transgenderism are presently manifesting themselves around the world.

In New York City we can now be fined up to $250,000 for using the wrong third-person personal pronoun. If a man asks us to refer to him as a 'she', or perhaps a 'they', or even something more exotic such as a 'ze', and if we decline and refer to him as a 'he', the result could be a catastrophic fine. Note that to refer to a man as a 'he' is to use the right pronoun whereas the legislation purports to punish people for using the 'wrong' pronoun. The legislation punishes people for using ordinary words in their ordinary way. What is that, if not an example of calling evil good and good evil?

Used by billions of people around the world (including young children), Facebook now allows us to choose from seventy-one gender identities, and if none of them resonate with us we can type in a customised one—meaning that, in theory, there are infinite gender identities available to us.

Meanwhile in Denmark, if we wish to change ('re-assign') our gender identity we need to fill in a form. Six months later we need to fill in a second form to confirm that we filled in the first form. And that's it. What used to be seen as a medical procedure is now deemed an administrative one, something that happens not on an operating table with a scalpel but in an office with a pen.

Lastly, the Justices of the Supreme Court of the United States recently decided they would hear the case of a teenage schoolgirl, Caitlyn 'Gavin' Grimm, who insists on being allowed into the boys' locker room at her school. An issue that ought to have been resolved in-house will instead be heard in the highest court in the land.

I don't know about you but to my mind these four examples are off-the-scale crazy. That, though, is the background to our discussion, just a snapshot of some of the weirdness that is swirling round our heads. It is fair to say we are living in interesting times.

What is Gender?

To begin, what is gender? This question needs to be asked because the subject can be extremely confusing. There are lots of contradictions in play, many different opinions coming from many different directions, and ample scope for talking past each other rather than making progress.

Much of the confusion comes from the fact that the word 'gender' means different things to different people. So, we are going to do ourselves a big favour and de-clutter the conversation so that we can see clearly into the heart of the matter. (The heart of the matter is what we will come to in part two.) We will de-clutter things by working our way through three different meanings of the word, comparing them to the legal meaning. Our focus needs to be on law for the crucial reason that man-made law—and only man-made law—has the power to impose its belief on us. For example, regardless of how we as individuals or groups of people use the word, we do not possess the power to force head teachers to allow boys into the girls' showers, whereas the state does.

Gender as Sex?

Our first meaning is that gender is just another word for sex. We fill in forms—either by hand or online—and they ask us for our 'gender', with the options generally being male and female. Given that those are the names we have given to the sexes it would seem reasonable to assume that sex and gender are one and the same.

But we are now starting to see forms that ask us whether we are male, female, or... something else. Indeed, Australia, New Zealand, India, Pakistan, Bangladesh, and Nepal each offer an official third option of some kind. Yet when it comes to sex there is no 'something else'. There are only two sexes, meaning that if the form is giving us a third option it is not asking us about embodied-ness. So, for legal purposes, does gender mean sex? Our answer has to be no, not only because of the emergence of a third option on some forms but also because more and more countries are allowing people to re-assign gender identity without surgery and without hormone injections — without diagnosis, even.

We have already mentioned Denmark, but we can also mention Argentina, Colombia, Ireland, Italy and Malta. Britain and America too look set to embrace this approach, with the emerging international gold standard for gender re-assignment laws being that they should revolve not around diagnosis and surgery but around self-declaration. It is as though when a man says he is a woman, his saying so is the very thing which makes him so.

What does all this mean? It means that if the Danish government is using 'gender' to mean sex, and if it believes that it is possible to re-assign gender without having an operation, then the Danish government believes that it is possible to change sex without, well, changing sex! From a legal perspective, no, gender does not mean sex.

Gender as Psychological Sex?
A second use of the word is that gender signifies not our sex but our psychological sex. It is a person's inner sense of himself or herself as either a male or a female. This is a nice manageable idea, as there are only four possible permutations: a male who perceives himself to be male; a male who perceives himself to be female; a female who

perceives herself to be female; and a female who perceives herself to be male.

Again, though, this use of the word does not match up with law. In June 2016, an Oregon judge allowed resident Jamie Shupe to legally identify himself (yes) as neither male nor female. We also see 'both' listed as a possible gender identity despite neither 'neither' nor 'both' being a sex. Gender-as-psychological-sex does not explain how it is possible to identify as 'neither' or 'both', let alone how we get from two gender identities to seventy-one.

Nevertheless, this use of the word is important to be aware of as it is the way in which the word is used by many of the ideology's most vociferous opponents. In its position statement *Gender Ideology Harms Children* (updated August 2016), the American College of Paediatricians uses the term 'gender' in a consistent way, to mean a person's sense of himself or herself, defined in relation to sex — male and female. The ACP also takes a strong and welcome line in defence of children and against the notion of 'surgical impersonation of the opposite sex'.

Gender as Social Sex?
Having looked at gender as sex and gender as psychological sex, our third use of the word is social sex. This is the way in which feminists in particular use the word, to denote the socio-cultural manifestation of sexual difference, existing in the form of expected behaviours and appearances, i.e. stereotypes — things such as the idea that boys should have short hair and girls should have long hair; that blue is for boys and pink is for girls, and so on. On this reading there is a strong artificial aspect to gender. Feminists see it as a limiting construct, with women in particular being held back by it. The bottom line for feminists is that gender needs to be erased. It should be noted, then, that when we hear people

say, 'Gender is a social construct', they are not claiming that *sex* is a social construct. Rather, it is just another instance of the word being used in a different way.

Yet again, this use of the word does not correspond to the legal use. It is not at all clear why an identity defined in terms of a social construct ought to be recognised and protected in law in the first place. And why would feminists want the state to protect an identity defined in terms of a concept which they want to see erased?

However, a feminist perspective of the overall situation does provide us with some helpful insights, including the fact that feminists and the ACP have something in common. Take this quotation from Rebecca Reilly-Cooper, an analytical philosopher who has produced a lot of very good work highlighting the ways in which the present meaning of gender identity contradicts the established feminist understanding of gender. It comes from her essay *Gender is Not a Spectrum* (Aeon.co, 28th June 2016):

What is gender? This is a question that cuts to the very heart of feminist theory and practice, and is pivotal to current debates in social justice activism about class, identity and privilege. In everyday conversation, the word 'gender' is a synonym for what would more accurately be referred to as 'sex'...The word 'gender' originally had a purely grammatical meaning in languages that classify their nouns as masculine, feminine or neuter. But since at least the 1960s, the word has taken on another meaning, allowing us to make a distinction between sex and gender. For feminists, this distinction has been important, because it enables us to acknowledge that some of the differences between women and men are traceable to biology, while others have their roots in environment, culture, upbringing and education.

Here are two more quotations, both of them from the writer Sarah Ditum. The first is taken from a very long and very well received essay rather tellingly titled *What is Gender, Anyway?* (New Statesman, 16th May 2016):

This (gender) can be perplexing terrain, in which it's not at all clear that everyone is speaking the same language, although they might be using the same words.

And from an essay called *How Society is Failing Transgender Children* (New Statesman, 25th October 2016):

Remarkably, as I found out when I worked on a long feature on the subject, there isn't any agreement on what gender identity is or how it relates to the physical body. Which means that transitioning children are receiving an untested treatment for an undefined condition.

What do these quotations tell us? Well, firstly, they show that feminists acknowledge that the word 'gender' has other widely-used meanings (gender as sex and gender relating to language). Secondly, they make it clear that feminists are acutely aware of the fact that when it comes to newer uses of the word not everybody is on the same page. Thirdly, the quotations illustrate that although feminists and conservative American paediatricians use the word 'gender' in different ways to each other, the two camps are united by something good and powerful. They may not often be bedfellows, but in this instance both camps are alarmed at the way in which the modern understanding of gender identity is harming children.

In effect, feminists are saying to the state, 'You are getting gender wrong. Gender is a social construct, so how can it be related to a medical diagnosis? And why would anybody need surgery to change gender?' Similarly, the ACP is saying to the U.S. administration, 'You are getting gender wrong. Gender is our psychological sex, so surely any incongruence between sex and gender represents a disorder—one which can be treated only by treating the mind.'

As we work our way through the fog, it ought to be dawning on us that the state is not getting gender wrong at all. Rather, it is using the word in yet another way. But what is that use, if not sex, psychological sex or social sex?

So Many Meanings; So Much Confusion

Just before moving on to part two let us press pause and make a general observation about language. We are not in a situation of using the word 'gender' to signify an aspect of human identity plus, say, a brand of car, a kind of cheese, and a Pokémon character. In such a situation, our particular use of the word at any one time would be more or less obvious from the context in which we are using it. For example, if John were to say, 'I am having gender on toast for lunch' we would know he is not talking about eating his car, right?

But that is not the present situation. No, we are using the word to signify sex, psychological sex, social sex, and some kind of legal identity. All four uses occupy the same conceptual space: human identity. Is there any other word that not only has so many meanings but also has so many *overlapping meanings*? Does this not suggest that gender— as seen as an ideology—relies heavily on confusion and deception? Interesting times.

Sex and Gender

So, from a legal perspective, what exactly is meant by this phrase 'gender identity'? At the risk of sounding underwhelming, the question is difficult to answer because of the quality of the definitions available. Regardless of whether they are provided to us by law, by websites or by various organisations, the definition of a gender identity is always so very vague. It is frequently defined as being our 'inner sense' of ourselves as 'male, female, both or neither', but, as has been noted already, this cannot be referring to psychological sex. Winning the prize for the ultimate in vagueness, another not uncommon definition contends that our gender identity is—wait for it—the identity of our gender. It is not hard to see why such a definition is so inadequate: it goes around in circles. It is not a definition at all. It is the same as saying, 'Brexit means Brexit', and we all know the confusion being caused by that vagueness.

However, despite being unable to access a solid definition there is a neat trick we can fall back on, which is to define gender identity in terms of the properties it claims to have. (This technique is employed excellently by the aforementioned Reilly-Cooper in her YouTube presentation *Critically Examining the Doctrine of Gender Identity*.)

To explain what this technique entails, let us imagine that John tells us he does not know what the word 'elephant' means. Now, we could say to him, 'An elephant is a kind of animal,' or we could say something like this: 'Elephants are normally grey. You might find one in Africa. Elephants are bigger than a car but smaller than a house,' and so on. We could talk 'around' the fact that an elephant is an animal.

This is pretty much what we are reduced to when it comes to building a picture of what a gender identity is. For example, numbers: there is a particular number of sexes— two—whereas there is no particular number of gender identities. Likewise, in terms of sex we are referring to a physical identity whereas in terms of gender we are referring to an immaterial one—a state of mind. Two more properties: sex is given in conception whereas gender identity is chosen, and our sex cannot change whereas our gender identity apparently can.

A useful exercise is to imagine a vertical line dividing all things sex and all things gender: on sex's side of the line are words such as body, physical, two, given, and fixed, whereas on gender's side are mind, immaterial, infinite, chosen, and fluid. The discipline is to make sure that no word or idea ever crosses from one side of the line to the other. The beauty and value of looking at gender identity in terms of properties, then, lies in the fact that it allows us to put distance between sex and gender, in turn isolating gender and cutting down confusion. For as long as we can keep the two sets of ideas apart we can retain a sharp picture of their differences, with it quickly becoming apparent that sex and gender are not just different, they are in fact opposites.

Mind over Matter

Still, the question can be asked: why does any of this matter? Surely all that counts is that our legal identity is a legal recognition of our embodied identity? So what difference does it make whether the state believes we also have something called a 'gender identity', and that it can be changed? Here we reach the crux of the matter. Here is where the entire subject turns inside out. You see, according to law our gender identity is superior to our sex—hence the state now permitting us to choose which loo we use. The implications of this legal reversal of the body-mind relationship are almost impossible to exaggerate. In law, the visible given-ness of our body (sex) is deemed a less trustworthy indicator of identity than the invisible and chosen predilections of our mind ('gender').

At this point we have well and truly left behind the comforts of reality and have plunged headlong into the arms of an ideology for, in claiming to be superior to sex, our gender identity represents an active legal denial of our embodied identity as male or female. Thus, the state declares there to be nothing real about the human person other than that which we think. On this model of identity, our body itself can be only a state of mind.

The effect of the declaration is that we are 'downgraded' in law; legally considered to be less than who we really are. Put simply, gender identity is an attack on sex: if you are male this affects you; if you are female this affects you. This affects everybody. Expressed another way, the legal version of gender identity is a knowable lie, in that it contradicts a knowable truth, namely that our fundamental identity as embodied persons is a given identity which exists independent of our mind and just so happens to be signified through the word 'sex'.

From Psychological Sex to Psychological Gender

Note how far away we now are from gender as psychological sex. We have made a subtle yet devastating shift, from 'gender as the sex we think we are' to 'gender as the gender we think we are'. Yes, the notion of gender defined only in terms of gender makes no sense (I am just the messenger!), but the shift does something bizarre. It detaches (legal) gender from sex, and therefore from the body, and therefore from any objective reference point. The ideology in fact prevents us from being able to access any legal recognition of our embodied identity.

This shift is such a vital point to grasp that it both needs and deserves an analogy to help illuminate it. To that end, let us think about the relationship between the size of our feet and the size of our shoes.

Why do we wear shoes that fit? It is because of the presence of a norm: there is a normal connection between feet size and shoe size, with the latter determined by the former. The two ought to match. Likewise, there is a normal connection between the sex we are and the sex we perceive ourselves to be. The two ought to match. Now, suppose we think not about the size of our shoes but about their colour. Yes, we are still talking about shoes but, suddenly, we are no longer talking about something that has any normal connection to the size of our feet—there is nothing about John having, say, size nine feet that determines he ought to wear, say, black shoes.

The analogy works because the difference between shoe size and shoe colour (with regard to the size of our feet) is the same as the difference between 'gender as the sex we think we are' and 'gender as the gender we think we are' (with regard to our sex). When we shift from gender-defined-in-terms-of-sex to gender-defined-in-terms-of-gender, we continue to use the word 'gender' but, suddenly, we have detached the word's meaning from any normal connection to sex.

If we think back to the way in which the word is used by psychologists and psychiatrists, we can now see where all the confusion comes from. From the perspective of socially conservative paediatricians, when the U.S. administration instructs them to alter a child's body rather than his or her mind the state is saying the equivalent of, 'If your shoes are too big or too small you should alter the size of your feet,' which is crazy, right? Which is why the ACP thinks the state is crazy. But from the perspective of law something very different is being said. The state is saying the equivalent of, 'A child's shoes can never be the wrong colour,' which is right, right? As far as the state is concerned our gender identity *can never be wrong*.

Legal gender claims to have no connection to the body, so cannot claim to have any connection to the sphere of medicine—hence the relentless and bloodless de-pathologisation of transgenderism in law. The ideology is coming out from its hiding place behind the body. It is beginning to flex its powerful and purely legal muscles.

The legal reading of gender exists 'beyond' the binary of sexual difference, which explains the proliferation in the number of available gender identities. The severing of the link between subjectivity and objectivity also accounts for the hyper-fluidity of (legal) gender, as well as explaining why words such as 'male', 'she', and 'father' are now legally regarded to belong not to states of body (sexes) but to states of mind (gender identities).

How to Respond?

At the outset, we said we cannot know how to respond to something unless we first know what that something is. And now we know: going on the legal use of the word, our gender identity is a self-chosen and changeable identity defined without reference to our body. We also said that without knowing what we are responding to we cannot know why it warrants a response. And now we know: our gender identity is legally deemed to be superior to our sex, thereby downgrading us in law from somebody to 'somemind'.

But there is a third aspect of how to respond. After 'what' and 'why' comes 'who'. Who will it be that brings us into contact with this ideology? Will it be our own son saying, 'I think I'm a girl'? Will it be a colleague who is going through some kind of physical transition? Will it be the government instructing our local school to allow pupils to choose which set of showers they use, or insisting that we use ordinary words in new and extraordinary ways?

Our response to all things 'gender', then, has to be informed by the fact that we are dealing with a very messy overlap between two things, which for the sake of convenience we can term illness and ideology. As recently as twenty years ago, those persons who experience incongruence between sex and psychological sex referred to themselves as transsexual. Nowadays, people with that same incongruence tend to refer to themselves as transgender. They are being sucked into the orbit of the ideology. Without meaning to be too graphic, we can expect that in years to come certain men will look back and think, 'You mean to tell me I could have become legally 'female' without having that operation?' The ideology is leaving bodies and body parts in its wake.

One of the greatest points of contrast between the illness and the ideology is that transsexualism affects less than 1% of people whereas by virtue of downgrading us in law the ideology affects 100% of us. Whilst we should not interpret this as permission to turn our back on those people who experience genuine difficulty living in harmony with their God-given sex, we do need to accept that it would be a self-destructive error to concentrate all our resources and energy only on compassionately walking alongside the 1%. Our focus must fall primarily on the ideology. The soundness of this position can be seen by realising that the cultivation of a deeper understanding of the ideology in turn enables us more accurately to understand the position in which people who identify as transgender unwittingly find themselves. They are caught in the crossfire between illness and ideology; between the medical and the legal.

Sex Education?

A second group of people who are particularly vulnerable to the ideology are children, as they are less able intellectually to fend off ideas that make no sense. It helps here to stop and think about what we mean by *education*. When it comes to teaching children mathematics we expect schools to teach children the truth of mathematics, i.e. that it is a fixed structure which can be operated but not altered. Likewise, teachers are expected to tell children the truth of art, which is that, unlike mathematics, art is subjective. What, then, ought to be the content of sex education? It ought to be the truth of human sexuality: that the body is marital; that sexual behaviour is moral only within a permanent and exclusive sexual union (called a marriage); and that a marriage is inherently structured towards bringing about the procreation and rearing of children.

Instead, we see the implementation of a new and radical version of sex 'education'. (For a critique, see Family Watch International's documentary, *The War on Children: The Comprehensive Sexuality Education Agenda*.) The worrying aspect of this agenda is not so much what *is* being taught but what *is not* being taught: marriage and heteronormativity. Thus, the truth about the meaning of the body is being 'hidden' from children.

Today's problems exist not because we do not know enough about gender but because we have forgotten so much about sex. This might sound rather contradictory coming from somebody who has spent four years studying the notion of self-chosen legal identities but, yes, our emphasis should be on re-learning the nature and meaning of the human body made male and female, and on teaching it to children: the better their understanding of their given identity, the stronger their immunisation against the ideology.

Bodies and Words

An additional, very simple and effective step all of us can take is to follow the advice of Stella Morabito, an expert on the techniques of mass propaganda. We can stop using the word 'gender' when we mean 'sex', and in doing so attach our language more firmly to the reality of the body. Sex means something real, observable and measurable, whereas the only meaning of 'gender' that has any historical roots is its use in relation to language. This does not mean we should not use the word at all. Rather, it means we should aim to use it in the same way as all other words, i.e. accurately.

Likewise, sticking with the proper use of third-person personal pronouns conserves the relationship between language and the human body. So-called preferred pronouns (or 'gender pronouns') are a hall of mirrors: once entered into, the idea that each individual can invent his or her own pronouns is very difficult to escape from. Again, the effect of separating pronouns from bodies is an increase in the distance between our true identity and our words. Eventually, stripped of its words, our body falls into silence.

Natural Man versus Legal Man

Let us not be mistaken or naïve. At root, what we are witnessing is the worldwide implementation of an ideology which has the full backing of law. Indeed, the systematic, top-down rolling out of the ideology even has its own name: Gender Mainstreaming. (See *The Global Sexual Revolution: Destruction of Freedom in the Name of Freedom* by Gabriele Kuby.) If gender is a virus then gender mainstreaming is that mode of working whereby each part of the 'body' of law is forcibly infected. Gender mainstreaming is the wave by which all signs of sex and sexual difference are to be flushed out of the legal system. All the more reason to continue to speak in a way which recognises, reveals, and respects sex and sexual difference.

The ideology named Gender insists that each and every one of us learns to be a person in a new way. But if it is a new way it is not the old way, and if it is not the old way it is not the true way. So, if we once more visualise our vertical line dividing sex and gender, we can now add a few more pairs of opposite terms to our list. We can add true and false, and we can add creature (who recognises that he has a Creator) and self-proclaimed self-creator. We can also add freedom and whatever the opposite of freedom is.

To close, consider what the downgrading of the body in law does for the legal status of myriad aspects of our embodied identity. Let us take age as an example. John cannot be thirty years old without being a thirty-year old male. Similarly, he cannot be English without being an English man. That is to say, his body is his core identity, with all aspects of his identity being aspects of that core. Now, we cannot deny the truth of the whole of something whilst simultaneously clinging on to the truth of some part of said whole. So it is that to vaporise human identity in law—with our body being 'replaced' by our mind—is to convert all aspects of our identity from 'aspects of a core physical identity' to 'aspects of a core mind-based identity'.

In sum, if our body is without legal meaning then no dimension of human personhood can have any legal meaning. The 'new normal', then, is that there is no normal.

OTHER LGBT ISSUES

6

CHASTE IS THE NEW QUEER

Prof. Robert Oscar Lopez

Perhaps no term has caused greater misunderstanding than 'social justice'. To a certain brand of liberal, this denotes a commitment to human dignity in the area of economics and material living conditions, but a disregard for human dignity in the area of sexual ethics. To most Christians, 'justice' is a partner of 'mercy' and both fit in with a larger system of social obligations, which include compassion in the realm of economics but self-restraint in the realm of sexuality (summarised aptly as 'chastity'). Greed and lust are both, for example, among the seven 'cardinal' sins. The left's habit of separating greed and lust, vilifying the former while trivialising and excusing the latter, can be understood if one accepts the implication that economic injustices harm whole classes of people while lust is largely contained to the intimate sphere where harm is difficult to quantify, particularly between consenting adults.

The child emerges within Christianity, however, as an implicit challenge to the left's vision of social justice and a vindication of the conservative Christian view. The child is born from sexual intercourse and is captive to whatever social framework adults' sexual choices created. The child is also the quintessentially vulnerable being in a society and the measure of how just a society has become. Consider the pivotal quote from Mark 9:42: 'Whoever causes one of these little ones who believe in me to sin, it would be better for him if a great millstone were hung around his neck and he were thrown into the sea.' The child's impressionability and helplessness places a duty upon adults to keep the child from sinning. And what is 'sin'? Throughout the Bible, it is not merely economic oppression or judging one's fellows harshly. Rules about correct sexual conduct are voluminous, explicit, and enforced with extreme measures, even in the New Testament. In 1 Corinthians 5, as Paul addresses the problem of sexual misbehaviour in Corinth, he writes, 'I wrote to you not to associate with anyone who bears the name of brother if he is guilty of immorality or greed ... not even to eat with such a one'. One can certainly argue that economic injustices are not to be neglected, but one cannot do as many 'social justice' liberals do and downplay the impact of sexual excess, particularly on children who have to deal with the culture created by such excess.

Despite repeated efforts by LGBT activists to equate 'love' with toleration of sodomy, the New Testament provides clear definitions of love, which preclude sin and which demand that a respect for vulnerable children be observed. In 1 Corinthians 13 appears Paul's famed disquisition on love, so often recited at weddings. A reference to childhood, in bold, is included:

Love never ends; as for prophecies, they pass away; as for tongues, they will cease; as for knowledge, it will pass away. For our knowledge is imperfect and our prophecy is imperfect; but when the perfect comes the imperfect will pass away. **When I was a child, I spoke like a child, I reasoned like a child; when I became a man, I gave up childish ways.** For now we see in a mirror dimly, but then face to face. (1 Corinthians 13:8-12).

Included in this crucial description of love is a mandate to respect the transition from childhood to adulthood. In this transition comes an expansion to new forms of love unknown to people when they are very young, with sexuality being the most conspicuous new form.

To cultivate a just society, one must create a Christian culture that fosters a healthy transition from childhood to adulthood. This means an observance of proper boundaries and a respect for sexual limitations—ergo, the centrality of chastity as something much greater than a mere afterthought. Chastity is a lynchpin of any real social justice. Sexuality flows from culture; where bad sexual habits abound, injustice rather than justice flourishes. In this chapter, I will accept as a given that the left's commonplace attacks on 'neo-liberalism' reflect a sincere commitment to social justice. Nonetheless, I will challenge the left's common parlance about neo-liberalism to ask why chastity, so crucial to children's rights and to social justice in general, is so often misunderstood, ignored, or wilfully misrepresented in the left's discourse on neo-liberalism.

The fantasy of chastity's conspiring with corporate exploitation

Among many critics of 'neo-liberalism', a self-defeating fantasy surfaces again and again. It is a comforting but ultimately fallacious illusion that fiscal and social conservatives are united in the pursuit of globalised capital. The fantasy is not without basis but it is severely outdated and under-critiqued. In the 1980s, Ronald Reagan built a conservative coalition and drew disaffected Democrats to his side by promoting the notion of a three-legged stool: one leg was strong defence, one capitalism, and one social traditionalism. This three-headed Cerberus has lived on in the minds of Reagan's leftist detractors, symbolising a unified but destructive ideology against which the left needed to marshal its intellectual prowess. Since Reaganism was politically triumphant throughout the 1980s, the left turned largely to culture, arts, and academic scholarship to counter him, with the result that the latter's discourses configured caricatures of right-wing extremism and naturalised the mutual necessity of military, fiscal, and social conservatism. Writing in the *National Review,* Eliana Johnson invoked memories of Reagan's famous stool as she commented sadly on the political theatre of 2016:

Since Reagan's election in 1980, the GOP has been defined by social conservatism, fiscal restraint, and muscular internationalism. Mitt Romney dragged a three-legged stool around Iowa in 2007 to illustrate the party's three ideological pillars, telling voters that "our candidate has to be somebody who can represent and speak for all three legs of the conservative stool or conservative coalition that Ronald Reagan put together — social conservatives, economic conservatives, and defence conservatives". Unscrewing one leg at a time, he showed voters that without any one of these pillars, the stool would crash to the ground (Johnson, para. 2).

Johnson's article was entitled 'The Death of Reagan's Republican Party', which was a frank admission that things had changed dramatically and the three-legged stool was no longer real. Throughout 2016, key writers for this same publication—including Kevin Williamson, Jonah Goldberg, and David French—warned right-wing readers to stay away from Donald J. Trump, not only because of his allegedly unstable temperament but also, more importantly, because of his dangerous flirtation with isolationist and socialist ideas anathema to the right's self-image of small-government domesticity combined with muscular militarism abroad. In arguably the greatest rebuke to the right-wing intellectual class, their warnings and active attempts to sabotage Trump failed, and he won not only the Republican nomination but also the presidency. Conservative elites still romanticised Ronald Reagan, William F. Buckley, and the *National Review,* but in 2016, the world discovered that such elites spoke for very few people and certainly not for the masses of people with traditional values.

Johnson's requiem for Reaganism was timely. In broadsides such as 'Against Trump', a conservative manifesto authored jointly by twenty-two writers and published in January 2016, Donald J. Trump was roundly attacked by free-market conservatives for his ideas about trade and by neo-conservatives for his rejection of militarism ('Against Trump').[1] Nevertheless, his vision of tariffs and softer defence policy won him 81% of the white evangelical vote, even with his blemished personal life of divorces and sexual misadventures. While he likely lost evangelicals of colour, polls showed they did not prefer Clinton to Trump by the margins forecast prior to voting (Shellnut, paras. 2-3).

To millions of people who opposed same-sex marriage and abortion, Romney's message failed but Trump's succeeded. Why? Largely, one could infer, because Trump attacked globalisation and highlighted the economic plight of workers left behind by neo-liberal trade policies, especially in the Rust Belt states he flipped to the Republican column. Even Michael Moore's prediction of a Trump win in October 2016, while peppered with sarcastic insults toward Trump, listed his economic appeal to depressed labour in the Midwest as the first of five reasons Trump was sure to win (Moore, paras. 9-11). When the espousal of chastity coincided with neo-liberal trade policies, as one saw in 2012 with Romney's glorification of business owners, 'job creators', and 'makers' rather than 'takers', social conservatives stayed home in large numbers or voted for Obama so they could get health care. Trump appealed to social conservatives when he picked well-known evangelical Mike Pence as his Vice President, vowed to defund Planned Parenthood, and listed conservative names as picks for the Supreme Court. Social conservatives flocked to him, in defiance of the *National Review* and *Weekly Standard*. A mass of people, neglected for decades, saw greed and lust as interconnected problems in society and longed to join a movement that pushed back against the Sexual Revolution and neo-liberalism simultaneously. As I pointed out in an April 2016 column for *Federalist,* the false association between sexual anomie and racial justice amounted to white men falsely appropriating Martin Luther King's movement in the 1950s to rationalise their rejection of Christian rules about chastity. Norman Mailer, Arthur Miller, and Hugh Heffner were all part of this distorting effect:

Miller's 'Crucible' used the Salem witch trials as an obvious allegory for the repressions of creative people by Wisconsin Rep. Joseph McCarthy and the House Un-American Activities Committee. Miller's play reinforced the association in Americans' minds between sexually judgmental Puritans and their penchant for political persecution. Puritan Hester Prynne of Nathaniel Hawthorne's 'Scarlet Letter' was a returning spectre in the American conscience, a symbol of sexual heroism, the martyr whose defiance of oppression consisted of eroticism forbidden by snoopy matrons and emasculated hypocrites.

These strong messages converged in Norman Mailer's chronicling of the hipster movement. While maintaining some ironic distance from the hipsters in 'The White Negro', Mailer furthers the period's habit of framing radicalism sexually. Mailer implies that white male sexual transgression could be a revolutionary act against political repression, equivalent to black families facing fire hoses and bulldogs to enrol in white schools. (Paras. 4-5)

Multitudes of Americans saw the Sexual Revolution and neo-liberalism not as oil and water but as twin pillars of the same problem. The events of 2016 pose, therefore, a problem for queer theorists and left-wing dissenters. With respect to this problem, I can offer some particular insights even if I am an unlikely interlocutor for the current anthology. Though I organised anti-war protests in 2002-3 and voted for Al Gore in 2000 and John Kerry in 2004, I am not now, and have never been, a libertarian or left-wing intellectual. George W. Bush failed to win my vote because I disliked his economic and military policies even though I agreed wholeheartedly with him on social and cultural issues like abortion and sexuality. Eight years have passed since I was last published in *CounterPunch* and by now, it seems, nobody with socially conservative views can speak with legitimacy to leftists who may share an opposition to neo-liberalism in the economic and global sense. I am high on the list of global culprits compiled in the Human Rights Campaign's 'Export of Hate' and one of the few academics who joined Newt Gingrich in signing 'Scholars and Writers for Trump'.[2] Still, in 2016 both the co-editor of the volume published by England's Wilberforce Publications (*Jephthah's Children*) and the co-author of *Sunlight,* a play that premiered in London on November 11, 2016, were women rooted in the left (Brittany Klein and Michelle Shocked, respectively). I have never been able to extricate myself entirely from the leftist tradition, and I see our current political moment as an occasion for me to engage the left on the issue of neo-liberalism. Having fought in the trenches on multiple continents against the LGBT agenda, I have no desire to position myself as a moderate, a builder of bridges, or a seeker of common ground à la Russell Moore or Pope Francis. But as a Southern Baptist with Asian and Latino ancestry, having grown up with a queer mother, and having defined myself as queer for many years, I am a bogeyman who confounds the left as much as I infuriate it. For I am arguably more opposed to global neo-liberalism than most left-wing critics.

Like so many people with roots in the developing world, I identify both feminism and LGBT activism as neo-liberal and neo-colonial constructs implicated in cultural imperialism, racial oppression, misogyny, and class inequality. For almost a decade I have travelled in a discursive space that is half Gloria Anzaldúa's *Borderlands* and half Homi Bhabha's 'Third Space'. It is a place where I can see things that I know others cannot, but which I know are true. My career in the academy has been peculiarly turbulent because I trouble an assumption that matters a great deal to other academics: namely, the presumption that fighting against chastity means fighting neo-liberalism and that queerness is positioned against hegemony. Upon this assumption hangs, arguably, the entire raison d'être of queer theory. Within this fantasy, those who push for concentrated wealth among a global elite (and diminished freedoms among the global masses) are seen as morally equivalent to, and really allied with, those who value chastity and who consequently oppose extramarital sex and sodomy. Ergo, on that view, to fight against chastity is to fight against the ills of global capitalism.

One would be hard-pressed to find one definition of 'neo-liberalism', however, that naturally affirms the dissident left's yearning to fight chastity and global capitalism at the same time. Chastity limits and restrains the appetite for pleasure while global capitalism advances by manipulating and monetising consumers' appetite for pleasure of all kinds, including sexuality. In *Empire,* Michael Hardt and Antonio Negri summarise the main beast of neo-liberalism this way: it is

... the capitalist project to bring together economic power and political power, to realize, in other words, a properly capitalist order. In constitutional terms, the processes of globalization are no longer merely a fact but also a source of juridical definitions that tends to project a single supranational figure of political power. (9)

The 'neo' in neo-liberalism signifies different things to different critics, but invariably the prefix implies that there is something deceptive or unexpected about the way classical liberalism turned into a new 'global order', which camouflages militarism, exploitation, and totalitarianism behind ostensibly liberal concepts like 'multiculturalism', 'free trade', or 'a world without borders'.

Is neo-liberalism wed to chastity? Hardt and Negri's vision of an imperial, capital-driven neo-liberalism does not look considerably incompatible with the global movement for 'LGBTQIA rights' forwarded by global organisations like Europe's ILGA or the United States-based Human Rights Campaign. The latter group enjoys the patronage of vulture-fund scion Paul Singer and the backing of Lockheed Martin. The global nature of the LGBT movement may have had its roots in the well-documented transnational phenomenon of sex tourism, something that is difficult to define as resistance to neo-liberalism, since the tourists were largely rich white gays vacationing in tropical climes populated by poorer native populations. Perhaps queer theorists of the 1990s and early 2000s did not foresee the level of coordination between pro-LGBT advocates and the United States government when initially they defined queerness as antithetical to neo-liberalism and vice versa.

Chastity is easier to define than neo-liberalism or queerness. When defining chastity in a Christian context, clarity comes from Matthew 19, the passage in which Jesus strengthens the taboo against divorce: 'Haven't you read', he replied, 'that he who created them in the beginning created male and female?' and he also said, 'For this reason a man will leave his father and mother and be joined to his wife, and the two will become one flesh?' So they are no longer two but one flesh. 'Therefore, what God has joined together, man must not put asunder' (Matthew 19:4-6). The sex act is the merging of two bodies, who must not be separated once they have joined in intercourse. The rule against promiscuity and adultery is enhanced by a rule about sexual differentiation, by the Bible's multiple references to 'mother and father', not only in Proverbs but also in the fifth commandment in Exodus. Notwithstanding heroic attempts to legitimise homosexuality by 'progressive' Christians, the Bible's holistic vision of social relationships emblematises chastity as an ordering of sexuality along lines of male-female exclusivity and permanence, largely because such an ordering serves the obligations to both parents and children.

Chastity is a demanding, usually religious concept, which stipulates that sexual pleasure must be restricted to a man and woman within the confines of marriage. Feminists and queer activists generally dislike such a concept and work to discourage it from taking hold as a cultural norm, which is probably why so many left-wing critics of neo-liberalism are so insistent that anti-chaste behaviour amounts to politically resisting the neo-liberal world order. Queers have an obvious reason for disliking chastity since it precludes the main thing that draws them together, which is the willingness to find pleasure with the same sex and to resist taboos against homosexuality. The idea that chaste marriage oppresses women is more complicated. Many marriages in history took place within societies that generally disfavoured women, so feminists have some grounds to object that chastity co-existed with oppression of females, who often had to be married and had to be unequally burdened within their marriage, or else face scorn and even violent retaliation. There is no denying that chastity as a virtue was often imposed disproportionately on women, who were more often accused of violating it since they were the ones who got pregnant.

Yet by 2012 I witnessed a different landscape in which to understand the relationship between chastity and neo-liberalism. Having come out against homosexual parenting that year, I was invited to speak before a conference of the Love and Fidelity Network, an organisation that promotes chastity among students at various colleges. The event took place in Princeton, New Jersey. When I got there, I noticed that there seemed to be a large number of vocal, motivated women, and a number of mild-mannered, gentle males. Of course, most if not all were religious, especially Christian. I would be a guest speaker at many of these groups' meetings over the next four years, and generally I found that Christian women within such organisations had positions of power and respect. Though many of them would not describe themselves as feminists, they surrounded themselves with friends who would not allow men to speak disrespectfully about women. Men who behaved in sexually inappropriate ways were shunned. What I realised over the course of this work was that a parallel movement of female empowerment was slowly taking hold, mirroring all the aims of feminism except for feminists' rejection of chastity. Old-fashioned courtship notions actually made many of the women feel powerful. Rather than busying themselves with sexual arrangements, they found the time and space to pursue their careers because their studies and work were not disrupted with the drama of sexual controversies involving feckless men. Men who were part of these chaste circles understood they had to sacrifice their urges to a larger good that focused particularly on supporting and nurturing women.

The feminist rejection of chastity makes sense to some women but to many it runs counter to the kind of power they hope to exercise in the world and the kind of concessions they expect from men given the historical reality that all such social interactions occur in the aftermath of millennia of sexism. Chastity in its core essence imposes limitations on males as well as females. Men are forced to share their resources and commit to a shared life with one woman or face scorn and loss of social status, which blocks them from excluding women from their wealth and creating a social world with nothing but other men. In a world where the workplace, courts, and government have worked to eliminate discrimination against women, chastity would ideally keep men from offsetting the loss of their predominance in the civic sphere with increased domination in the intimate, domestic, and sexual sphere (either by replacing women in that sphere with men, or by refusing to commit to any long-term support of sexual partners in that sphere).

Consider the common assumption that fighting chastity would always be coterminous with fighting the modern capitalist state. The converse implication is that modern capitalism in its ugliest forms fears roving sexual pleasure and has an incentive to police transgression (*pace* free-trade and sex-positive parties, including pornography companies that fought against California's anti-barebacking Proposition 60). In *The Reification of Desire: Toward a Queer Marxism*, Kevin Floyd pictures queer practices as designed to 'counter the state' because queerness insists on 'legitimating the homosexual objectification of the body' and 'refuses to see promiscuity as inherently dehumanizing or shameful'. In the previous decade, Lisa Duggan argued in 'Queering the State' that queer politics came as a necessary defence against the dominance of conservative governance, which 'assumes the universality and normative superiority of marital heterosexual relationships, and positions homosexuality and bisexuality as immoral and sinful threats to family values'. Duggan's earlier iteration came during the presidency of Bill Clinton, a powerful white man who orchestrated the North American Free Trade Agreement (NAFTA) but still found himself attacked by the conservatives in the wake of his false statements about adultery with an intern half his age. The claim that the critiques of Clinton's sex life stemmed from pro-corporate sexism and racism were, in retrospect, more than a little strained, but they made perfect sense to intellectuals of the nineties, perhaps because the habit of yoking racism and antifeminism to homophobia were already de rigueur by then. In acquainting readers with the conservatives she deploys queerness against, Duggan states, 'It is clear that the strategies of the religious right go well beyond the simple articulation of homophobic, racist, and antifeminist sentiments.' Duggan was open to varying forms of queer activism, as long as they shared one kernel: 'a strategy of public display and cultural intervention – a strategy positing a shifting, oppositional constituency'.

Queerness was defined consistently by what it was not. It was not gay and lesbian politics, which was too vulnerable to ghettoising and anti-intellectual identity politics. It was not conservative or judgmental about how people pursued pleasure. But it was not a simple exercise in marketing and consumerism either, because it was articulated in a post-Cold War West in which governments opposed sexual deviance and governments were capitalist. The whole system of queer politics depended on the assumption that sexual deviance undermined governments and the capitalism driving them.

It is intriguing that the fantasy of 'fighting neo-liberalism by fighting chastity' has continued unquestioned for as long as it has. There is something ripe for contestation in the assumption that people with unusual sexual proclivities are naturally opposed to racism, sexism, or global capitalism; or that everyone racist will automatically want to make life miserable for people who defy chastity. Aristocracies and oligarchies are famous for their sexual decadence—consider the tawdry picture of Havana's orgiastic decadence, as depicted in Luis Cabrera Infante's novel *Tres Tristes Tigres*. Remember the luridness of Petronius's *Satyricon* or the rakes of eighteenth-century epistolary novels like *Clarissa* or *The Coquette*.

Yet one ought not to mock the fantasy of 'fighting neo-liberalism by fighting chastity', because it spoke powerfully to my generation as we emerged from college. As someone who jumped into queer theory wholeheartedly in the late 1980s, raised by a lesbian mother and defying, in my mind, every state-imposed stricture I could imagine, these formulations made sense to me as the Reagan era drew to a close. I was young and Puerto Rican without resources in New York City. My mother had died and her sexuality caused a great deal of confusion about the money she left to her children, which resulted in my financial struggles and exposure to discriminatory urban conditions. Having no experience of having been anything other than the powerless victim of other people's mistakes, I took seriously and believed the comforting notion that all my problems were being inflicted on me by the same wealthy, racist classes who both judged my parents for their sexual transgressions and blocked me from the kind of career advancement my peers seemed to be enjoying.

Now, Ronald Reagan has been dead for more than a

decade. It is 2017 and I have sired children as a result of my pursuit of pleasure with a woman. Having seen that my decisions would have enormous impacts on two powerless human beings who did not ask to be born my children, but were, I simply cannot look past all the gaps and contradictions in queer theory. The whole exercise has collapsed. I have seen how chastity is a socially responsible state of being, which gives the vulnerable members of society protection against oppression and mistreatment by the state as well as people in the world at large. Against such a backdrop, sexual gratification is simply selfish and inconsiderate to others. If opponents of neo-liberalism expect millions of powerful wealth holders to restrain themselves out of concern for the welfare of others, I cannot see how these same critics can reject chastity, which is the most obvious and relatable example of people restraining themselves out of concern for the welfare of others. To topple neo-liberalism requires a strong commitment to the notion of sacrifice, yet rejecting chastity means rejecting the requirement to sacrifice an intimate matter—mutual pleasure—for the sake of a higher good. The inclusion of queer politics in the fight against neo-liberalism looks increasingly untenable and even fatal.

Whether I changed or society changed, I look at what Lisa Duggan and her cohort envisioned at the dawn of queer theory and I see a *Titanic* heading toward a very large iceberg of reality. People who rebel against chastity are rarely revolutionaries against sexism, racism – much less neo-liberalism. They are more often than not sexually desirous people who do not like being told what they can and cannot do. If they do not like to be told who, when, and how to have sex, they are probably not going to like being forced to constrain their civic activities in order to accommodate the specific demands of people of colour, women, or any other group of subalterns. When I went to the United Nations to present on children's rights, and demonstrated that the gay parenting movement was impinging on centuries of international law designed to protect women and children, especially those from poor backgrounds or from less powerful nations, I saw very clearly that queer theory's assumptions did not ring true. Gay white men who wanted a patrimony like their straight male counterparts were eager to find cheap and expendable surrogate wombs to gestate captive children.

Intellectual fashion has carved out a strange common ground where the West's queer activism remains broadly unchallenged within the West's dissident left-wing intelligentsia. According to critical ethnic studies, the settler colonialist 'heteropatriarchy', to borrow from the lexicon used by anti-colonialists like Andrea Smith, is threatened both by workers' revolution and individuals revelling in sexual transgressions. This allows the same activists who call for the overthrow of the global capitalist order and imperialism to champion liberal disregard for sexual taboos like those against extramarital sex, homoeroticism, and anal sex.[3]

The fruit of this fusion is a sequence of assumptions: 'Greed' stems from 'bigotry', and 'bigots' are de facto racist, sexist, and homophobic simultaneously. The benefit of grouping fiscal and social conservatives together for rhetorical purposes is obvious: It makes the movement against neo-liberalism simpler to define and allows for a disparate range of groups who might otherwise quarrel and splinter to function as 'allies'. How else would one unite the anti-racist activists who fight against neo-colonialism, for instance, and gay white men who want to contract non-white poor women to birth children who will love and obey them in the same way biological children of heterosexuals love and obey their parents?

The fantasy of neo-liberalism's sexism and homophobia carries a number of downsides. Some movements need the perfect enemy. It is irresistible, and perhaps lucrative, for the left to envision racists, homophobes, sexists, and capitalists as all the same people, which in turn debilitates the left's ability to fight neo-liberal forces when they are cloaked in the terms of the Sexual Revolution. In November 2014, *Federalist* contributor Stella Morabito and I delivered a joint speech at Catholic University, on children's rights. The latter for us include three basic human rights: the right of every child to be born free rather than bought or sold, the right of every child to their mother and father, and the right of every child to his or her origins. While the three rights conform to many principles that leftists could not historically disavow—anti-slavery, anti-settler-colonialism, anti-eugenics, and anti-genocide—these rights also conflict with every means available to a same-sex couple desirous of children to raise as their own. Rather than present this as a diatribe against sodomy, we presented photographs of a conference in which students created exhibits about the history of family ties in literature: mother-daughter, father-daughter, mother-son, father-son, as well as sibling relationships. If homosexuals wished to take this personally and object to the conspicuous silence about same-sex couples' parenting of children, they were entitled to infer as much, though we did not showcase that aspect of our scholarship (Lopez and Morabito).

Prior to our arrival on campus, we were informed by the leaders of the Catholic Anscombe Society that hecklers were planning to protest our speech as anti-gay. The queer protesters made good on their threat. When Ms. Morabito and I spoke at Catholic, arguably the most conservative of Roman Catholic universities, we were heckled by several people who shouted, 'Racist, sexist, anti-gay, Christian fascists go away.' This occurred only two months after the

Human Rights Campaign, the world's largest organisation championing LGBT rights, listed me as one of the twelve most dangerous 'exporters of hate' in a report called 'Export of Hate'.

What in our presentation was racist or sexist? What in it was fascist? From where came this mantra of *racist, sexist, anti-gay,* which were indissolubly merged in the popular discourse? Out of respect for the supposedly timeless role of intellectuals in crafting complex readings of culture, one could refrain from blaming 'the left' for such a bizarre outburst by noting that thinkers like Andrea Smith and Jasbir Puar are removed from the chanting oversimplification of the hecklers at Catholic University. Yet the silence among elite left-wing intellectuals about the obvious affinity between neo-liberal capitalism and the LGBT movement leaves much room for questioning whether the intellectuals against neo-liberalism have failed to disseminate their message or, more damningly, failed to notice or give sufficient voice to a pro-chastity position steeped in resistance to the racism, sexism, colonialism, and exploitation typically associated with neo-liberalism.

Much of the presentation I gave in November 2014, for instance, showcased the research that would be published five months later in *Jephthah's Daughters: Innocent Casualties of the War for Family 'Equality'*. The latter book included multiple chapters on the harm done to women by commercialised surrogacy and gamete trafficking, a chapter on slavery and children's rights, a chapter on the 1978 law against Native American cultural genocide, a chapter on eugenics, a chapter on the moral hazards of transracial-transnational adoption, multiple chapters on the harm done to gay males by the gay marriage movement, a dozen chapters on the corruption of academia, and two dozen chapters on the damage inflicted on children in vulnerable communities.

The introduction of the book includes this paragraph:

The discredited logic behind slavery, cultural genocide, and eugenics snuck back into the zeitgeist, under the noses of the progressive critics who usually felt most superior to the slavers, settlers, and Nazis who practised those historic evils in earlier times. Resources for serious social-justice movements—such as women's rights, economic aid to the global poor, critical anti-racism, sexual assault intervention, and refugee assistance—shifted from urgent flashpoints toward hubs of wealthy professionals seeking fulfilment in their personal sex lives.

Speaking only for myself, I can embrace the label of 'anti-gay' because groups like the Human Rights Campaign have defined 'pro-gay' as necessarily dismissive of children's rights to be born free, to their mother and father, and to their origins. The objectionable part of the hecklers' approach was their mania about yoking anything anti-gay to racism, sexism, and fascism. In the reception following the speech, the hecklers hounded me until Ms. Morabito and I left, at which point they continued to scream epithets down the hall at us. Surprisingly, one white student tracked me down as I rushed to our car, telling me he was a far leftist, who agreed with my critiques of the globalised LGBT movement. He assumed that I was allied with the work of Lisa Duggan, a far-left professor at New York University. This student, perhaps too young to have been fully indoctrinated in the vocabulary and categories of the anti-neo-liberal left, thought my message was actually similar to the ideas espoused by the author of *Sapphic Slashers*, a nominee for an award from the Gay and Lesbian Alliance against Defamation, which had blacklisted me on its Commentator Accountability Project list the year before.

The naiveté of the sympathetic student is telling. While unthinkable to seasoned scholars, there is an unexamined mutuality in the views of far-left critics like Lisa Duggan and the right-wing championing of chastity. The notion of chastity and neo-liberalism merging in a Reaganist neo-liberalism can by now be described as a 'fantasy' because said connections are utterly false. First, people who fight against chastity—notably, pro-choice feminists and queer activists—rely upon a definition of free pleasure as a good, transformative tendency in itself, which is not only compatible with but supportive of neo-liberal visions of a consumer-driven free market. Second, there are real alliances between libertarians and anti-chastity groups, which are scrupulously ignored by scholars in neo-liberalism. The connections, for instance, between the pro-queer Human Rights Campaign and economic concerns like Lockheed Martin or financiers such as Paul Singer and George Soros, are so damaging to a conception of homophobia linked to neo-liberalism, that scholars who refuse to address this are remiss in their mission.

Queer theory was born a quarter of a century ago. It was a supposed counterweight against the entrenched gay and lesbian movement, which by the early 1990s already presaged some tendencies that left-wing scholars perceived as toxic. While there was a healthy cacophony among people who identified as queer theorists, there was a consistent idea within the field of positioning queerness as counter-hegemonic, anti-assimilationist, and essentially Marxist. In broadsides issued by academics against neo-liberal oppressors, for instance, a litany often presents a host of causes that are ostensibly arrayed against global hegemons. Take, for instance, a recent document that circulated, entitled, 'A Statement by Feminist Scholars on the Election of Donald Trump as President of the United States'. A call to action unites feminists from all around the world to fight, among other things, a specific model of neo-liberalism:

> As a community of feminist scholars, activists and artists, we affirm that the time to act is now. We cannot endure four years of a Trump presidency without a plan. We must protect reproductive justice, fight for Black lives, defend the rights of LGBTQIA people, disrupt the displacement of indigenous people and the stealing of their resources, advocate and provide safe havens for the undocumented, stridently reject Islamophobia, and oppose the acceleration of neoliberal policies that divert resources to the top 1% and abandon those at the bottom of the economic hierarchy. We must also denounce militarization at home and abroad, and climate change denial that threatens to destroy the entire planet.

Among the signatories are more than a few prominent people famed not only for feminism but also for queer studies: Judith Butler, Jasbir Puar, Medea Benjamin, Mary Louise Pratt, and Hazel Carby. This statement echoes innumerable declarations across the academic 'left' (if such a thing can be presumed to exist), yoking many different political issues together and placing them squarely against neo-liberalism. The problem is that this style of pamphleteering has far outgrown its historical relevance. There is no more three-legged stool and many gay people are counted in the corporate headquarters of a globalised economy. If the left cannot see this and re-assess their view of 'LGBT' as a common cause with social justice, the left will probably be unable to thwart its march toward obsolescence.

Notes

[1] In the second paragraph of the now-infamous 'Against Trump', the conservative objection to Trump's economic leftism is placed front and centre by the editorial board: 'The real-estate mogul and reality-TV star has supported abortion, gun control, single-payer health care à la Canada, and punitive taxes on the wealthy. (He and Bernie Sanders have shared more than funky outer-borough accents.)' ('Editors', para. 2).

[2] The full text of both open letters endorsing Trump can be found at: http://scholarsandwritersforamerica.org/

[3] Scott Laura Morgensen summarises the scholarly link between settler colonialism and heteropatriarchy in this review of Andrea Smith's work: 'By arguing that settler colonialism is a root of heteropatriarchy, indigenous feminists call for settler colonialism to be challenged in all feminist criticism and for a critique of heteropatriarchy to be centered in all indigenous movements. Indigenous feminism thus moves beyond self-representative organizing by indigenous women to present a distinctive critical theory of colonial and heteropatriarchal power in both indigenous and settler societies. In the process, and as Andrea Smith explains in her work reviewed here, indigenous feminists' defence of indigenous sovereignty methodologically undermines the heteropatriarchal and colonial form of the modern nation-state and redefines indigenous nationality on indigenist, feminist, and decolonial grounds that link national and transnational activisms.'

Works cited and Web Resources consulted

Clifford, Stephanie. 'Raid of Rentboy, an Escort Website, Angers Gay Activists', *New York Times* http://www.nytimes.com/2015/08/27/nyregion/raid-of-rentboy-an-escort-website-angers-gay-activists.html?&moduleDetail=section-news-2&action=click&contentCollection=N.Y.%20%252F%20Region%C2%AEion=Footer&module=MoreInSection&version=WhatsNext&contentID=WhatsNext&pgtype=article&_r=2

Duggan, Lisa. 'Queering the State', *Social Text* 39 (19), 1-14.

'Against Trump', *National Review* (January 21, 2016) http://www.nationalreview.com/article/430137/donald-trump-conservative-movement-menace

Floyd, Kevin. *The Reification of Desire: Toward a Queer Marxism* (Minneapolis: University of Minnesota Press, 2009).

Lopez, Bobby and Stella Morabito. 'When the Stepford Queers Come to Catholic U', in *Federalist* (November 25, 2014). See embedded YouTube video. http://thefederalist.com/2014/11/25/when-the-queer-stepfords-come-to-catholic-u/

Morgensen, Scott Lauria, Review of *Christian Right: Gendered Politics of Unlikely Alliances,* by Andrea Smith, *Signs* 36:3 (2011), 766-776.

Shellnut, Kate, 'Trump Elected President, Thanks to 4 in 5 White Evangelicals', *Christianity Today* (November 9, 2016).
http://www.christianitytoday.com/gleanings/2016/november/trump-elected-president-thanks-to-4-in-5-white-evangelicals.html
Two publications that can provide backup to the question of Paul Singer and Lockheed Martin funding the Human Rights Campaign:
http://www.washingtonblade.com/2013/11/06/controversy-over-hrcs-international-push-paul-singer/ (on Singer)
https://www.arktimes.com/ArkansasBlog/archives/2015/05/18/lockheed-martin-is-a-company-that-stands-for-lgbtq-rights-how-about-in-arkansas (Lockheed Martin)
Citation about the issue of who opposed Proposition 60 in California:
https://ballotpedia.org/California_Proposition_60,_Condoms_in_Pornographic_Films_(2016)
Concerning the Andrea Smith reference (on heteropatriarchy):
http://www.weldd.org/sites/default/files/andrea-smith.pdf
Reference to the hecklers at Catholic U:
Reference to the manifesto of feminists against Trump:
docs.google.com/forms/d/e/1FAIpQL.../viewform?c=0&w=1
https://soundcloud.com/militant-de-lenfant/80-feminists-against-trump

7

SAME-SEX PARENTING EQUIVALENCY?
A PERSONAL PERSPECTIVE

Brittany Klein

Same-sex parenting is a kind of child abuse that we have not even named yet. Sexual orientation and gender identity are creating a new type of orphan that will need to be recognised and protected. The ideology that underpins same-sex parenting denies children the most basic right and biological facts: the truth that everybody has a mother and a father. For the child raised in a same-sex household it means being raised in an ideology based in the adult sexual preference that did not create you.

At this point, for many of us, the adult children of LGBT, the arguments in favour of same-sex parenting feel glib, cynical, steeped in contemporary trends, social failures and progressive guilt.

The most-used tropes evoked are single mothers and divorce. Heterosexual sex still creates children. And despite all the misuses of the word 'discrimination', same-sex sex does not make babies—this does not mean we give people's children to other people because they have a piece a paper, a bank account and a mailing address. This argument is a deflection tactic that draws equivalency between children of divorced parents or children of single mothers and children of same-sex parents. The default rhetorical device used to frame same-sex parenting is as just another rung on the social progress ladder and hence a 'lib no brainer' (as LGBT argues – just like blacks and the civil rights issue).

Not to harp on too much reality too often, but we know that the expression 'single mother' does not mean that the child's father is not in the child's life. It just means the mother is not married to him. And, even in bad situations, that, in and of itself, does not exclude the possibility of the father in the future. On the other hand, same-sex severs any possibility of a relationship with at least one of the child's parents and forces the rest of society to betray and erase children's basic human rights in order to provide children for a grand social experiment. As in the dystopian novel *Never Let Me Go*, maybe it makes some people's lives better. But there is still no humanity to be had in the project.

Those who deny a child either a mother or a father are not operating from what is best for the child. They operate from 'entitlement' shored up by the distortions of postmodern identity politics — but there is no civil right to other people's children, or their DNA or their wombs.

Despite the lofty claims of love and tolerance, LGBT always employs bigotries that align perfectly with the same bigoted elitist values ('nice house, good neighbourhood' – read 'rich and white') that they lambast others over. The 'single mother' in LGBT hands often raises their favourite spectre of 'bad mother unworthy of her own children', the 'junky-whore mother' or the 'teen mother'. This gay misogyny, paired with the conviction that children are a commodity (meaning: if you want them it means you deserve them and somebody had better provide them), makes up the doctrine of entitlement that underlies 'LGBT parenting'. It is adult-centred. Wanting a child — even deeply — will not make you a better parent than the parents of the unplanned child. That notion, that 'want', is the hallmark of consumerism, where people swap 'want' for 'deserve'.

Throughout human history, people *wanted* a daughter and got a son or the other way—that's parenting. And for all their snipes about single mothers and how much better than them they are, let's be honest, single mothers are not trying to force the child to live some lie of immaculate conception as supported by media. They do not march down the street waving the single mother flags in G-stings squirting people with penis water guns. There are no organisations with paid activists sending death threats to their children whenever a child says they want a father full-time.

No matter how much the 'single mother' term is deployed to degrade women, an unplanned pregnancy demands sacrifice, and there is much to be said for parents who have sacrificed. These arguments also demean children—you know those creatures that come from sloppy heterosexual sex. It is not subtle calling other people sluts and whores, breeders who do not deserve their own children. It follows that an ideology which is demanding, entitled and self-centred precludes selfless parenting. It is all about *them* — same-sex parents who sever the child from at least one biological parent and then demand the child's unquestioning affection. What is the name for this new cruelty? Not equality, not love.

In service to the cause, public adult relationships have been turned into a kind of political theatre to prove to the world 'all samey' or 'love is love'. That exasperating cliche bleeds into other areas. Living your own lie is one thing, it is entirely another to demand that the children live adults' lies too. For the kids there is no escape because at this point — since there is an entire movement with an adjunct industry of LGBT doctors, shrinks, resorts, clubs and teachers — more and more adults who are not the parents also see the child as a piece of property that only exists to swear their allegiance to the sexual identity movement.

For young children who are not even sexual, who do not even know or care where babies come from, dividing the world into heterosexual and LGBT is harmful because they cannot grasp the division. Even so, it has to be enforced. As adults, we know it is a specious division invented for political reasons. On even the most basic child-centred level, adults' sexual interest and identity should not be the controlling theme of any child's life, nor the organising defining principle of the home. Yet so many of these children are trained, coached to defend 'gay' on cue. They know how to impress adults: be appealing to their 'progressive' egos. For the adults there are a lot of immature and distorted emotions and motivations at play, and a lack of empathy—this world is a punitive place for the child.

The adults' sexual identity as the pervading theme explains their preoccupation with issues such as the sexual education curriculum, so called 'safe schools' and 'anti-bullying'. Should a five-year-old be weighing in on whether or not the kindergarten teacher is straight or gay? Yet this is how they are taught and how it is demanded that they divide the world. Should a young child be forced to pay attention to adults' sexual attractions, adults' sexual desires which are, simply put, adult sexual pleasure? Demanding that children be cognisant of adult sexual urges and acts is not progressive, nor is this some highly evolved new-found freedom. They have not unlocked the shackles of an archaic, puritanical discriminatory practice — it is child abuse. It invades children's inner lives and deprives them of a childhood and, more significantly, their own identity.

For all of human history there are relative normative distinctions that have divided people (or bound them) based in some objective reality—historical, geographical, ethnic, economically rich and poor, old and young, black and white, but never by what people want to do behind bedroom doors and with whom it feels the best. Read through the actual narratives of people raised in these homes to see high rates of drug abuse, sexual acting out, suicide attempts, and the stories of those kids thrown out of their homes on to the street. The LGBT spin (denial to the power of 10) is 'rare exception' or 'junkie birth mother', or worst, the 'defective child'.

Consider why LGBT groups have thousands of youth centres and groups set up for the LGBT children of other people, yet they purposefully have nothing for their own children that are abused in the LGBT community and they do not police themselves. To hear them tell it, there is zero abuse in the LGBT homes. Really? How perfect are they? Alarm bells should be loud and clear. Most heart-wrenching is that they will protect the adult abuser and not the child. Worse, they will in fact collectively punish the victim and isolate them. What are the statistics of children in same-sex families concerning depression, suicide, drug abuse, sexually acting out? Anyone who thinks it does not happen is very wrong.

But it does not end in childhood. As both a social and a political movement, LGBT is a dysfunctional, abusive culture, steeped in narcissism and poised to harm anyone who believes that marriage is between a man and a woman, or who believes in the basic tenets of any of the world's main religions, or is a free speech advocate. In general, the sexual and gender identity industry has an unhealthy preoccupation with children. We see this in the 'safe schools' and so-called 'anti-bullying' programmes.

There is something shameless in a movement that uses kids – this is something that can't be explained, and people don't want to see it. The long con seems so blatant to me that I still have trouble accepting people who consider themselves both intelligent and acting out of good will who never questioned the whole media campaign. Are we to believe all those children that just felt compelled to write to a Supreme Court justice to let their mothers marry each other? Because a marriage certificate is what keeps kids up at night?

There is no statute of limitations or expiration date on what LGBT activists do to people who speak out. Their children seem to draw particularly vicious responses. Threats of violence are *de rigeur*. I became the target of a group of men connected to certain male-dominated organisations which have deep pockets to keep up harassment and hit many targets. Dead animals are left on one's driveway; one's kid is threatened. I was stalked. My employer was contacted over and over and over to harass them and demand that I be sacked.

It has been over two years, and I am still in awe of the reality—what we have sunk to, and what is considered political advocacy now in the hands of LGBT, including killing a child's pet, let alone that major national and international organisations for LGBT rights can support and pay people to stalk and threaten me, and that others launch attacks on my professional life as well as on family members.

Here is a small slice of what they did to me, for the record. They tore through personal information to use against me and my family. Then, after I became a target, I was cyber stalked, hacked, and they put my address out on the internet, contacted local activists, and so I was stalked and threatened endlessly by a tag team of 'gay adult male activists'. To say I lived in terror is an understatement. If people only knew the actual extent of what they do – the threats, the defamatory lies spread out over every aspect of a person's life! If they did know, then they might realise how abusive and unbalanced and dangerous these folk are, and not exactly what one would consider 'parent material'.

Yet these are tactics they use in parenting. If you find that hard to imagine, ask yourself what other group has ever done what they do in the first place. They harassed over seventy of my co-workers and contacts with a series of defamatory emails meant to publicly humiliate me, discredit me and get me fired. In some deeply unhinged creepiness they sent my parent's partner's obituary to the entire University department. That not only was an act of cruelty but also a thinly-veiled death threat. The ironic part was that the detailed obituary in fact confirmed in print what I said about the deep problems with same-sex parenting and the LGBT movement. Still not satisfied, they contacted the President of the University. Then, wonder of wonders, a student, out of the blue, accused me of stealing his cell phone and texting sexual obscenities to his mother. The problem with that little falsehood was that I have a visual impairment and can't text. He later recanted.

They sent repeated demands that I be sacked . . . or else. They contacted editors and publishers with whom I had long-term professional relationships. They contacted people I teach with. They bragged on open internet forums how they used their LGBT connections at my job at Wittenberg University in Ohio and had made sure I would never work again. Imagine my shock (I'm kidding) when the only people able to observe my teaching were the activists they contacted and the faculty head of the LGBT group on campus. Even so, they could not refute a single thing I said and became verifiable liars and monsters trying. More professional gay activists contacted my family members at their workplace and then tried to bribe them into publicly calling me a liar. They were looking for people willing to dish dirt on me. They attempted to sabotage my financial life in ways that were a reminder of the attack on conservative organisations that were attacked when a gay activist who worked for the IRS illegally disclosed information about donors. My house was vandalised, my car was vandalised, and my garden. Then they threatened my child and published the name and address of the person who baby-sat for me, to let me know they knew where to find her. They may have broken laws when they interfered with amicus briefs and lied to officers of the court to discredit me and get my amicus brief disqualified. I often wonder how many people that signed on as allies did so naively, or were paid off, or were blackmailed and threatened. Again I ask: what other group has done this to other people and to their own children? Think about it. The leopard does not change its spots. These men worked for the same groups that were founded by serial child rapists, men whose crimes were well known and covered up to the public.

Every child raised in LGBT has stories, too many, embittered by spite and narcissism, of those that raised them, and punctuated by the control and the humiliation tactics. You learn to live differently. For me, the most tellable happened over my first Fall break from University. On the phone I lied to my mother and told her that I had to study all weekend for a big history test. While I had school work, I did not have a history test. When classes resumed that Monday, my advisor and mentor told me he needed to speak with me. So on Wednesday I went to his office in the Fine Arts building. As I wandered around the office, he said that a call came in to one of the Dean's offices. He then said that I was reported for cheating on my history exam. I was blindsided. I don't think I said a word. I just started weeping. I knew I would be expelled. Cheating was serious. Not only would I be expelled, I also would then have no place to live or no student aid. For me it was school or homelessness. I did not defend myself. In those moments my life was over. That was exactly how I felt and what I believed. That is where I was raised.

Even though my mother could be charming and smart, and I did love her and she loved me and we did have many good times and shared appreciations, she was not to be trusted – not ever. This was and is something so entrenched in the community, a shared psychopathy that has been politicised and made socially acceptable in the echo chamber of identity politics. Now of course there are people who are islands of sanity, but what has created the success of this movement is such tactics of lies and threats. This is what makes this an anomaly.

Needless to say, the talking points we hear from the sexual and gender identity community are factually, historically, biological fabrications of political connivance and leverage – straight-up propaganda. Forcing them on other people, other people's children specifically, is like being forced to join 'The LGBT Peoples Temple of Sexual and Gender Identity'. It demands adherence to adults' sexual identity. Heterosexuals don't do that. And for what? The ignorant pay out the progressives and get to feel progressive, sophisticated and superior.

No matter how many laws are changed, no matter how much they shame and degrade the poor, the Christians, the single mothers, and no matter how much they push the narrative in schools, in the media — and no matter how many the hoax hate crimes, fake news and suicide threats—it still is not true that they have the right to deny children's basic rights. And for such highly evolved 'nuance' people, truth must mean something? Well, maybe not.

Think about what it means: being made your whole life to play 'pretend' for adults who are self-involved enough to make this demand in the first place. What do we feel when we accept these ideas? Progressive; smarter. Does someone feel more generous when they accept the notion of same-sex parenting? Children do not vote and they have no money. People so desperately want to be 'on the right side of history'. That place is a big vanity mirror where they will look better than the next guy. Demanding to control the future while claiming it as a historic legacy is a hallmark of totalitarianism.

Let's not confuse sex and love. Sexual freedom has been the LGBT number one priority up until recently. The LGBT community is well known for parties and cruising. Love? Not so much. Charity? Not at all. We don't exactly see LGBT rescue teams rushing to places with humanitarian aid. Their time is better spent tracking a Christian baker down and potentially putting their livelihood at risk. All this is under the cover of the teenage rhetoric of rainbow and unicorns. 'Love is love' has morphed from silly teen girl platitude into the wholly disingenuous and sinister. Get real! Bad parents 'love' their children. Stalkers 'love' their victims. Men who kill their wives 'love' them. 'Love' is not some magic salve, and sexual identity certainly isn't. Love is a pleasure and not always an equal one. We have the lover and the beloved — most people, given the choice and some honesty, would rather be the lover than the beloved — not equality. The overly romanticised notion of 'falling in love' has always been a marketing tool and propaganda, all the way back to the 'Art of Courtly Love'. People 'fall' into wells or off cliffs — is such 'falling' really a good thing? The truth is that we can *choose* to love and *learn* to love and *grow* to love. That is how arranged marriage works, and in fact most people on the planet are in arranged marriages. In the West we are just too locked into what is called in academic and leftist circles 'colonialism'. We can control our emotions. We do it all the time. Historically, and worldwide, 'in love' or 'sexual attraction' have never been a requirement to get married, and they certainly are not requirements for most of the world population — all those poor folk that LGBT hold in contempt and disdain as 'backward' not 'progressive'. Most of Asia still does arranged marriages as does much of the Muslim world and Africa. LGBT has cornered the market on a kind of imperialist bias that talks a lot about 'love'. If we are honest we respect the unspoken knowledge that those in arranged marriages will grow in love and learn about integrity, solace and perseverance. They marry to make a family for the children. That is wonderful and real. The children do not care if mummy and daddy are head over heels in love or sexually attracted to each other. Children care if they are there and nurtured by the people who made them. The children live in the family, not in the adults' marriage.

Laws being enacted which are based on claims about love display the emotional maturity of a twelve-year old doodling hearts and flowers on her notebook, lacking the perspective needed. Lawmakers are out of their depth and they are pandering. What it takes to keep these lies going is too high a price. Children are born with an innate need and a basic human right to a mother and a father. Children benefit from a mother and a father in ways that two adults of the same sex can never match. Simply put, children are 'born that way'.

We want to forget conveniently that often parenting is about sacrifice, not proving to the world you can role play some virtue signalling of 'You be the mummy and I be the mummy'. Then, for evidence of the falsehood, the movement demands all kinds of fraudulent legal documents, falsified birth certificates that say a child has two mothers or fathers — that is the stuff Orwell warned us about.

Many people who have lost their jobs and business because of this group can tell you that the same-sex marriage movement is filled with treachery because there is something deeply and profoundly treacherous about sexual supremacy, based in the state securing (mostly men's) sexual pleasure over the human rights of children, people of faith and others who have a shred of decency and honesty left. Marriage 'equality' is to society what an affair is to a marriage. Some marriages survive the betrayal, others don't. What it does is to legalise and document the primal wound for many children. It assaults human rights, religious freedom and parents' rights, all of which are of greater importance to more people for far longer.

At the core of all this are people who, no matter how many walls they fill with pictures of Disneyland vacations, or how much they write and talk of that moment, frozen in time, of smiles and ice cream cones, it is just that — a moment sealed and framed as part of a surface. People need to look up to see the wide implications, and then look down to see the smaller ones. The whole movement uses children as both a cover and shield. Kids are cute, small and pull in emotions that we would not have for fifty-year-old white guys in a dress, either wanting to adopt or claiming they are a twenty-four year-old pin up girl.

The social delusion that supports a same-sex couple having a new-found right to someone else's child is linked to the social delusion that men can become women, and both use children as the thin end of the wedge. What we are not supposed to notice is that accepting 'gay' as such actually means also accepting the reality that both a man and a woman are needed to make babies.

Finally, same-sex parenting points up a kind of strange disassociation and contradiction. Question: is not the demand for children in and of itself admitting that something is very empty and there is not enough to sustain the same-sex marriage? What's with the pretend families? What's with acting as if so many kids are not harmed and denied their basic human rights? Why is the LGBT movement so very invested in the denial of basic reality? As someone raised in the LGBT community by a lesbian mother, I can say it is not out of what the average person (with only a few destructive impulses) considers 'love'. Perhaps, if children are what is so wanted, maybe what is actually wanted is heterosexuality? If that is the case, would it not be better for adults to begin to be honest instead of demanding that society create a new form of human trafficking that now includes other people's children, wombs and their DNA?

8

WHO'S EDUCATING WHOM?
THE REVERSAL OF THE PARENT/CHILD
RELATIONSHIP

DANIEL MOODY

I would like to begin with a quotation. This comes from the American economist and political philosopher Thomas Sowell:

> Each new generation born is in effect an invasion of civilization by little barbarians, who must be civilized before it is too late.

I think there is a lot of truth in that quotation. The barbarians must be civilised, or else civilisation will become barbaric. We recognise that the natural family unit acts as a brake, so to speak, preventing the dear little monsters from becoming big and not-so-dear monsters.

The downside of the quotation is that it could be said to give the misleading impression that institutions such as marriage and family are mere human inventions, created only to combat the 'problem' of feral children.

Marriage and Family

In truth, marriage is a gift from God. It is something given to us in creation. Marriage is a possibility flowing out from the difference between male and female. So, rather than thinking of marriage as being a legal institution, or slightly more accurately, a social institution, we should go deeper still and recognise marriage to be what it really is, namely a natural institution.

One way of coming to see this more clearly is to think about two kinds of otherness. Firstly, at the individual level, each of us as male *or* female 'points' towards an otherness: another sex. Heterosexuality, then, is not a state of *thinking* or *doing*, chosen by 98% of us. It is instead a state of *being* that applies to 100% of us. Secondly, at the level of a union—as male *and* female—our bodies point towards not another sex but another time. Maleness and femaleness point 'through' each other to the future—to children and family.

So it is that the vows exchanged by a bride and groom are promises not only to each other as individuals but also to the truth of the nature of the relationship into which they are freely entering. This 'promise to the future' necessarily extends up to, and includes a promise to, any children that their marriage may be blessed with.

As *The Book of Common Prayer* has it, 'First, it was ordained for the procreation of children, to be brought up in the fear and nurture of the Lord....'

This recognition of the inherent link between marriage and children was attested to earlier than the *The Book of Common Prayer*, in Augustine's three goods of marriage—children, faithfulness, and sacredness—and has been recognised since then, enshrined in international law from both directions, as it were: our international Rights mechanisms recognise both that men and women have the right to marry and to found a family, and that children have the right to know their parents.

The Transmission of Knowledge

The 'fear and nurture of the Lord'. I like that word, 'nurture'. I like the way two of its meanings play off each other: to nurture, as in to *feed*, and to nurture as in to *educate*. It evokes a lovely image, almost as though knowledge is something which we can spoon into the mouth of a child.

Marriage and family are, then, the natural pattern by which truths about human personhood are securely handed on from one generation to the next. We could perhaps say that a society with a strong marriage culture is a society which simultaneously both respects its own past and arranges its affairs so as to prepare for its own future. Indeed, Pope Leo XIII described the family as being 'a society very small... but none the less a true society'. Seen in this way, each generation is something like a member of a team in a relay race, with knowledge being the baton and family being the mechanism which facilitates and ensures a smooth changeover.

Now, if we try to imagine a world in which knowledge is not transmitted from generation to generation, that imagined world is all too bleak. Imagine, for example, that each and every generation has to discover for itself the laws of physics, say, or how to build a piano—or even that such a thing as a piano is possible.

It should go without saying that there are many areas of knowledge which we can and should pass on within the family setting. For instance, teaching children how to read, write, and count, teaching them about health, morals, and so on. But underneath all of these there is a prior area of knowledge: identity. *Who* is it that the parents are teaching to speak and read and count? *Who* is it that they are educating about health and morals? The answer, of course, is somebody: a male or a female. It is their son or their daughter.

Parents cannot teach their son to *be* male since he already *is* male, cannot *not* be male, and therefore always *will be* male. But parents can—and, I suggest, must—teach him what it *means* to be male: his future as a man; perhaps as a husband; perhaps as a father.

Dropping the Baton

So far so good, but what happens when something goes wrong? What happens when a generation drops the baton? What happens when a generation of children are not handed on a sufficiently strong understanding of themselves as male and female? The generation I am referring to is, of course, our generation.

I want to make two points here, neither of which should be interpreted as being a comment about any particular individual. Rather, the points are offered so as to present an overview of the general direction in which society is heading.

Firstly, we have to admit that whilst this generation will almost certainly grow up into adults who have an impoverished understanding of themselves, they will also almost certainly figure out how to make babies. Let's face it: we are good at making babies; not so good at making families.

Secondly, if the men and women of this impoverished generation *do* become parents—whether it is within a marriage or without—they may be poorly positioned to hand on vital truths to their own children. Yes, they may well be able to teach their son how to read and write and count, but what about identity?

Where a father and mother are insufficiently equipped with an awareness of the truth of their own bodies, how can they resist their own son when he looks up at them, smiles sweetly, and announces... 'I'm a girl'?

The parents are powerless to react in any way other than to accept 'her' claim.

So begins the reversal of the parent/child relationship. So begins the parents' 'education' at the feet of their own child.

Obviously, there are many things adults and parents can learn from children: how to look at the world in wonder again; what it is like to be frightened; what it is like to be responsible for somebody's very life. But is the interchange-ability of maleness and femaleness something adults should be 'learning' from children? I don't think so.

Contagion

As a phenomenon—that is to say, at the general level rather than the individual—transgenderism has a distinct whiff of contagion about it. As early as the year 2000 the American bio-ethicist and philosopher Carl Elliott wrote a thought-provoking essay titled *A New Way to Be Mad*, in which he posited the idea that the mere *description* of a condition can make it contagious. In other words, the *possibility* of having a new condition—be it Attention Deficit Disorder, Body Integrity Identity Disorder, and so on—tends towards people becoming somebody who claims to have that condition. The suggestion here is that society itself can will illnesses into being.

Applying this to issues of sex and gender (regardless of what we take that word to mean), we can say that the rise in the number of children identifying as transgender is in part a symptom of a lack of self-knowledge among us adults. This lack expresses itself in an inability to give to a child that which properly belongs to him or her: self-knowledge of self-identity.

A spark which in days gone by would not have become a flame has today turned into an inferno raging across Western civilisation. Surely if a child is owed anything in this world it is access to the truth about the meaning and nature of his or her body. Surely a child deserves to be protected from his or her inner-lurking barbarian.

9

POLYAMORY AND THE HUMAN GOOD

JAMES D. LOPEZ

What is polyamory? A lot of people are not familiar with the concept of *polyamory*, but in the subculture—whether in the U.S. or abroad, polyamory is a thriving reality. Polyamory is a practice involving multiple romantic or sexual relationships at the same time with every member's complete knowledge and consent (Haritaworn et al., 2006). It is important to differentiate polyamory from other kinds of relationships. Polyamory should not be confused with other non-monogamous structures such as open-relationships or swinging. In the former, each partner in a relationship has the liberty to have sex with other people, whereas in the latter, couples usually join other couples for the purpose of having sex. There are many other kinds of non-monogamous relationships, but open-relationships and swinging tend to be the most popular alongside polyamory relationships.

In polyamory, unlike other non-monogamous relationships, every partner involved is committed to each partner. Individuals in polyamorous relationships are known as 'polys'. A poly-relationship is short for a polyamorous relationship or union. Typically, poly-relationships tend to be composed of three individuals, but there are poly-relationships that involve more than three people as well. There is no limit to how many people can be in a poly-relationship as long as there is commitment, full knowledge, and consent amongst everyone participating in the relationship. In almost every poly-relationship, there are primary partners and secondary partners. Primary partners tend to be the husband and wife or main boyfriend and girlfriend (sometimes they are the ones with children in the household). The secondary partners tend to be other polys that were invited to join the poly-relationship by the primary partners. Unlike individuals in open relationships, individuals in a polyamorous relationship have a strong commitment to each other, and they take honesty and faithfulness as serious components for their relationship to thrive.

Reasons for participating in polyamorous relationships
In her book *The Polyamorists Next Door: Inside Multiple-Partner Relationships and Families*, polyamory expert and activist Elisabeth Sheff lists six common reasons people give for participating in polyamory. The most common is because this poly-arrangement 'meets more needs'. In other words, the poly-arrangement provides a platform that allows for deeper fulfilment because there is more than one partner in the relationship, therefore the various needs that a human person has are more likely to be met because there are more people involved in the relationship, which minimises the likelihood of neglect. Second, individuals participate in polyamory because the poly-structure provides a capacity for more love, which polys find lacking in a monogamous relationship. Third, polyamory offers sexual variety, that is, polyamory offers individuals the potential for more 'sex with different kinds of partners'. The fourth reason is to have a 'larger family with more love to go around, outside of the framework of one man, one woman'. The fifth reason is because it feels more natural to them. And the sixth reason is that it satisfies an individual's desire for freedom and rebellion. Polyamory is 'something they select because it fits

with their desire for freedom of self-expression and rebellion against social convention,' writes Sheff.

For many polys, marriage is nothing more than a social construction; marriage was invented to tame humanity's sexual drive. Monogamy is not considered the default practice for many in the polyamory community because it reduces human complexity and sexuality to fit instrumental social relationships and norms (Robinson, 1997). For many polys, however, sexual pleasure is not the most important factor, rather the presence of others is what matters most. More people in a committed relationship means individuals will not be neglected, as tends to happen in monogamous relationships, argue some in the poly-community. In a poly-relationship, if a partner works a lot, there is usually another partner available to meet the needs of the one who stays home.

Polyamory as an alternative to monogamy

One Google search using the term *polyamory* will yield all sorts of news coverage highlighting the poly-lifestyle or will take you to polyamory dating sites or societies. Polyamory is a growing trend in the popular news media. In 2014, the *New York Post* published a story with the headline: 'Married lesbian "throuple" expecting first child.' The throuple's marriage, though not legally recognised, was celebrated because each partner made and exchanged vows with each other. This 'throuple' is now expecting a child. The youngest member of the 'throuple' and the biological mother, Kitten, said, 'The three of us have always wanted kids and wanted to grow our family.' It is not the case that every poly-relationship or poly-family has or wants children, nonetheless there are many children growing up in these family structures (Anapol, 2012; Sheff, 2015). In 2013, CNN ran a headline story, 'Polyamory: When three isn't a crowd', describing the polyamory experience from the point of view of a poly-family. The poly-family in this story covered by CNN was also a 'throuple'. This poly-family consisted of Billy, his wife Amy, and their third partner, Jeremy. Although Billy and Amy are legally married, Billy, Amy, and Jeremy are not in a legal union because 'throuples' have no legal recognition in their residing state, but nonetheless live together and do everything that any couple does together, including sleeping together.

Polyamory is considered an alternative to monogamy because polyamory is just one lifestyle or preferred union amongst many others that consenting adults choose. Just like some people prefer hamburgers over a salad, for many people in the poly-community polyamory is their preferred relationship or structure. Preferring polyamory over monogamy does not necessarily entail that monogamy is inherently bad. The key point that the poly-community try to get across is that people have an array of diverse preferences, and as such, have a right to pursue what fulfils them insofar as no harm is done to others.

The six primary reasons that Sheff lists for why individuals participate in polyamory can be summarised in the following manner: Human beings are different, therefore many people will inevitably have diverse sexual and romantic desires that monogamy itself cannot satisfy, principally because it is a social convention aimed at keeping human behaviours and actions in an undeviating form. But is it the case that because there is mutual consent and no harm is being done, therefore any action is necessarily right or good?

Freedom and the Human Good

What is the purpose of human freedom? Is the purpose of freedom to choose or pursue whatever we want? The norm that is spreading across our culture is that as long as there is mutual consent, and no harm is being done, individuals have a right to engage in any kind of activity they deem worthwhile. This is the same kind of logic that undergirds the arguments for the legalisation of same-sex marriage. If the relationship between two individuals of the same sex does not hurt anybody, why should anyone prevent them from getting married? The problem with this is that human freedom is misunderstood.

In order to have a proper understanding of human freedom, it is essential to comprehend what is good for human beings. Unless there is a prior understanding of the good, or the good life, freedom will be used to justify any kind of action or behaviour, even irrational behaviour. Humans have freedom of the will. But is it the case that just about anything that is chosen will necessarily be good for humans? The clear-cut answer here is an emphatic 'no'. There are many obvious things that are *bad* for human beings. For example, deciding to give up drinking fluids and eating is bad because it will inevitably lead to death. It is not a social convention that giving up drinking fluids and eating leads to death, it is a concrete fact of reality. Taking the life of an innocent human being is also considered morally impermissible because there is something wrong about taking away an innocent human life.

What then is the purpose of human freedom? There is an array of fundamental human goods that when pursued, lead to human beings flourishing as the kind of beings they are. Some examples of fundamental human goods are life, knowledge, and friendship (Oderberg, 2000). Life is a fundamental human good because without life nothing can be accomplished. Without the proper care and maintenance of the human body, humans will not be able to flourish because they will experience all sorts of set-backs due to sickness or malnutrition. The pursuit of truth or knowledge allows people to avoid error and helps them understand the world and many of the affairs therein. Friendship, like life and knowledge, is also a basic component of human flourishing. Through the establishment of friendships and even marriage, people strengthen their social skills and, amongst many other things, learn how to better cooperate with others. Human freedom *really* exists to allow people to pursue these basic components of human flourishing. Without there being basic components of human flourishing, law-making would be an even tougher process.

The Polyamory structure distances the needs of children
Though it is true that not every poly-family has children, and polyamory as a relationship has no legal status or recognition yet, it is the case that there are many poly-families with children in their household. In the final section that follows I argue that the new family structure of polyamory is not good for children because this structure intentionally deprives them of their right to grow up with their biological father and mother.

It is true that there are countless children growing up in single-parent households. And it is also true that there are many children being raised by step-parents. However, just because step-parents are common, and there are a lot of children in adopted and foster care homes, does not justify the claim that the nuclear family is not necessary for a child's well-being. Sheff writes, 'In a sea of single parents, divorced, remarried, and cohabiting adults with children they bore or adopted, poly families may appear to be just another blended family.' (Sheff, 2015). The problem is that children in single-parent households do not choose to be born into these broken families; broken families are tragic and affect children, yet, amongst the poly-families that do have children, children are intentionally placed in these new family structures.

Polyamory further distances the actual needs of children, namely growing up with their biological parents.

Some scholars argue that polyamory is a good thing—that it is empowering for women and helps children to be more tolerant of others. According to Elisabeth Sheff,

Polyamorous relationships provide women with more power in their relationships, allows some women to reject sexual and gender roles, allows sexuality to be viewed as a source of unity among some women, and empowers women's high sexual drive. (Sheff, 2005)

But what about the children? Deborah Anapol, a clinical psychologist, interviewed adults in multi-adult relationships as well as children reared in those contexts. In her view,

Polyamory breaks down cultural patterns of control as well as ownership and property rights between persons and, by replacing them with a family milieu of unconditional love, trust, and respect, provides an avenue to the creation of a more just and peaceful world. By changing the size, structure, and emotional context of the family, the personalities of the children developing in these families naturally change. Children learn by example. (Anapol, 2012)

The unspoken—and untrue—premise implicit in this argument is that permanent, exclusive, faithful heterosexual marriages are based on nothing but a masked urge to 'own' another human being, as if he or she were an object. Ironically, such objectification is actually more in line with the nature of polyamorous relationships, in which a partner is used to fulfil certain emotional needs but is supplemented by one or more others. Rather than committing to a single person in all of his or her complexity, weakness, and strength, those who choose polyamory try to acquire a collection of attributes that will contribute to their own enjoyment and perceived well-being.

Many attempts to defend polyamory rely heavily on the idea that such relationships bring deeper fulfilment to adults. If this is true, the argument goes, then they should be more able and willing to provide emotional support to their children and the children of their romantic partners. But such arguments ignore data on outcomes for children with non-biologically related parental figures. As David F. Bjorklund and Ashley C. Jordan write in their article titled, 'Human Parenting from an Evolutionary Perspective',

> In studies across a wide range of cultures, stepparents have been found to spend less money on education and food, and to spend less time interacting with their stepchildren than their biological children... The single best predictor of child abuse is the presence of a stepparent in the home. In fact, the risk of even unintentional deaths, such as drowning, is greater in stepfamilies than in intact or single-parent families.

There is no good data on the parenting of 'throuples', or at least not conclusive data, yet. But at least one parent in a 'throuple' functions quite similarly to a step-parent. And the data gathered from stepfamilies illustrate the point that social science has repeatedly confirmed: on average, children fare better in a household with their married biological parents. Divorced and remarried parents or parents engaged in polyamorous relationships may find romantic fulfilment through such arrangements, but they do not necessarily create 'a family milieu of unconditional love, trust, and respect'.

Gender, Parenting, and Childhood Development

Children have the right to be loved and nurtured by the two parents who helped create them. Children have the right to live in an environment suitable for the raising of a child, not one that is only concerned with the fulfilment of adult desires. If the evidence shows that the best environment for children is the one provided by their mother and father, why willingly challenge this fact of life? Why not promote it instead?

In the article The Effect of Gender-Based Parental Influences on Raising Children, psychiatrist and distinguished fellow of the American Psychiatric Association Scott Haltzman observes:

Parenting styles correlate to biological differences between men and women. Women, compared to men, have higher levels of oxytocin—the hormone responsible for emotional bonding—and oxytocin receptors. Oxytocin serves to calm anxiety, reduce motor activity, and foster an increase in touch. In contrast, testosterone—present in men at levels tenfold higher than women—is correlated to an increase in motor activity in infant boys and may be responsible for higher levels of physical activities in men compared to women.

Fathers and mothers both matter, particularly if each can parent in a style that reflects their gender role. The evidence suggests that efforts should be made to educate society at large, and parents in particular, that gender differences in parents are real, and, rather than be extinguished or ignored, they should be embraced.

Fathers and mothers are different, and advances in our understanding of human physiology increasingly reveal the biological factors behind those differences. The male and the female come together as father and mother to bring complementary gifts to their children. Just because children cannot choose their family structures does not mean that adults will not harm children by deciding to disregard the structure of natural marriage. With polyamory, society is embarking on a vast and sweeping social experiment. The primary victims of that experiment will be children.

References

Anapol, D. M., *Polyamory in the Twenty-first Century: Love and Intimacy with Multiple Partners,* Lanham, MD: Rowman & Littlefield (2012).

Haritaworn, J., Lin, C., & Klesse, C. 'Poly/logue: A Critical Introduction to Polyamory' (2006). *Sexualities*, 9(5), 515-529.

Oderberg, D., *Moral Theory: A Non-consequentialist Approach*. Oxford: Blackwell Publishing (2000).

Robinson, V., 'My Baby Just Cares for Me: Feminism, Heterosexuality and Non-monogamy'. *Journal of Gender Studies*, 6(2), 143-157 (1997).

Sheff, E., 'Polyamorous Women, Sexual Subjectivity and Power', *Journal of Contemporary Ethnography*, 34(3), 251-283 (2005).

Sheff, E., *The Polyamorists Next Door: Inside Multiple-Partner Relationships and Families,* Lanham, MD: Rowman & Littlefield, Inc. (2015).

Wilcox, W. B., & Kline, K. K., *Gender and Parenthood: Biological and Social Scientific Perspectives*. New York: Columbia University Press (2013).

10

THE BIBLE AND THE RAINBOW

John Nolland

Prolegomena

When the lesbian and gay community claimed the rainbow for their cause, they claimed it as a symbol of hope. And their hopes have been realised beyond all expectation. But things have moved on, and now we have LGBTIQ, one for each colour of the rainbow, and more on the way. But political and cultural success does not establish the rightness of a cause.

For Christians the central question remains: what does God think of all this? And as Bible-focussed Christians we turn to Jesus and the Bible for God's steer on these matters.

Many have been trying to persuade us either that the Bible is out of date on these matters, or that it doesn't actually mean what on the face of things it seems to mean.

I lecture an MA hermeneutics class on Rom 1:26-27, one of the important New Testament sex passages. I introduce them to a dozen new approaches to Romans 1, all of which give a green light for homosexual relationships today. All the clever new approaches can be adequately answered, but they do knock people's confidence.

Having so many views around is like having a whole lot of smoke in the air. With all the smoke around nobody can see anything very clearly. People don't need to be persuaded of another view; they only need to be no longer quite sure.

And so we have confusion. And while the greatest sexual revolution the world has ever known is going on before our eyes we sit on the sidelines, unsure about it all.

The voices of those who can speak with confidence and conviction about how good the new sexual freedoms are find little resistance. And soon we have a brave new world.

I want to show that for Bible focussed Christians, sex is and always has been profoundly important, and must remain so. Indeed precisely because traditional Christian sexual morality is now so contested in our wider society, a focus on sexual morality is more important than ever.

1. How important is sex for (a) Jesus and the Gospels; and (b) Paul?
2. What kind of sex really matters (a) for Jesus; and (b) for Paul?
3. Why is the New Testament so concerned to strictly channel human erotic activity?

1 (a) How important is sex for Jesus and the Gospels?

The thrust of Jesus' mission was certainly not to clean up the sexual ethics of his people. Compared to how much Jesus talked about the kingdom of God, he did not talk much about sexual morality. But before we make too much of this, we need to see it in relation to the scale of investment in other aspects of morality in Jesus' teaching.

One kind of index is to compare how often he talked about sexual matters with how often he talked about other matters. Nobody doubts that Jesus cared passionately about love and had a profound concern for the poor.

In the Gospels there are fourteen references to love. *Agape* and the cognate *agapao*, noun and verb respectively for 'love', are the words used to press the claims of mutual love. There is love of enemies (Mt 5:44; Lk 6:27, 35), love of neighbour as oneself (Mt 19:19; 22:39; Mk 12:31, 33; Lk 10:27) and the call to love one another (Jn 13:3435; 15:17).

Similarly, there are thirteen places where Jesus' concern for the poor and their needs comes to direct expression. The Greek term involved here is *ptochos*. There is good news to the poor (Mt 11:5; Lk 4:18; 7:22; cf. Mt 5:3; Lk 6:20), giving to the poor (Mt 19:21; Mk 10:21; Lk 18:22; 19:8), Lazarus as poor (Lk 16:20, 22) and a banquet for the poor as a directive and in a parable (Lk 14:13, 21). We should also add the material in the parable in Mt 25:31-46 that identifies care of the needy as a key priority and also the reference to the hungry being filled in Lk 6:2. So we have thirteen direct references plus a couple of extras to concern for the poor.

So what about references to sexual morality? Here my count is twenty-six references to matters concerning sex. Here the vocabulary makes use of two Greek roots: *moich-* and *porn-*. More about these later, but the first deals with adultery and the second with all forms of sexual activity in the wrong place. The *moich-* family of words is used nineteen times in the Gospels, though three of these relate to the phrase 'sinful and adulterous generation', where the usage might be metaphorical (but which would nonetheless still indirectly reflect disapproval of adultery). There is adultery of the eye and heart (Mt 5:27, 28), divorce as adultery (Mt 5:32 (x2); 19:9; Mk 10:11, 12; Lk 16:18 (x2)), the adulterous generation (Mt 12:39; 16:4; Mk 8:38), adultery as a sin from the heart (Mt 15:19; Mk 7:22), adultery as forbidden by one of the Ten Commandments (Mt 19:18; Mk 10:19; Lk 18:20) and adultery as sin, but to be forgiven (Jn 8:3, 4).

The Gospels have Jesus using the *porn-* word group seven times. There is *porneia* in the exception clause in the divorce materials (Mt 5:32; 19:9) and in the list of sins from the heart (Mt 15:19; Mk 7:21); and there is *porne* uses with negative overtones of prostitutes (Mt 21:31, 32; Lk 15:30).

So, while Jesus commends the virtue of mutual love with fourteen uses of the *agap-* word group and commends or models concern for the poor with about the same number of uses of *ptochos* and a few further times in other ways, he speaks against adultery and other sexual immorality, explicitly or implicitly, with no less than twenty-six uses of the key terms. Maybe sexual issues did matter quite a bit to Jesus!

Sometimes it is claimed not only that Jesus did not speak much about sexual ethics, but also that, when he did, it was generally in response to questions (implying that this indicates that this whole area was not particularly on his agenda). How does this stack up with the evidence we have just reviewed? Strikingly, only in the case of the woman caught in adultery (Jn 7:53-8:11), does anyone other than Jesus himself put sex on the agenda.

There are other indicators that the Gospel Jesus might have thought that sex really mattered. Within the Gospel of Matthew the antitheses in chapter 5 (vv. 21-48) have a strong claim to be putting forward matters that are of particular importance to Jesus: here he defines his vision of goodness over against alternative options. And we find that two of the six antitheses are devoted to matters of sexual ethics (vv. 27-32). Concern for the poor does not feature, and love (of enemies) turns up in one, admittedly in the final and climactic antithesis.

Jesus' vice lists echo but go beyond the Old Testament Ten Commandments. The expansion involves a prominence for the sexual and making sure that forms of sexual sin other than adultery are brought into view. When Jesus wants to make the point that evil proceeds from the heart, two of the six items on the Matthean list (Mt 15:19) have to do with sexual behaviour: 'For out of the heart come evil inclinations, murder, adultery, fornication, theft, false witness, slander'. Matthew has abbreviated and reordered the Markan material to correlate with the Ten Commandments. All his items relate to the Ten Commandments and are dealt with in Ten Commandment order from murder to false witness (the preceding commandment of the Ten has been dealt with earlier in vv. 3-6). Making a clear link with the Ten Commandments underlines the importance of these matters. But we should also note that he is expanding the language from the adultery commandment to ensure that it will be understood to embrace other forms of sexual misconduct. Mark has a longer list of twelve items (Mk 7:21-22). The first four are concrete acts and the following eight are orientations of the heart—which no doubt are seen as producing specific acts of wickedness. Among the concrete acts Mark's version highlights the sexual by placing *porneia* at the beginning of the list of four and *moicheia* at its end. In Mark's version fully half of the list of concrete acts (two of the four) are sexual acts. The link with the Ten Commandments is again important in the accounts of the rich young ruler. Jesus tells him to keep the commandments and highlights some of them (Mt 19:17-19; Mk 10:19; Lk 18:20). To underline the link they basically come in Ten Commandment order, though honouring of parents has moved from the front to the end of the list.

In the light of these observations it seems hard to deny to the Gospel Jesus a profound concern for sexual ethics. Such a concern did not define his ministry, but to move sexual ethics to the sidelines is hardly in line with the values of the Jesus of the Gospels.

1. (b) How important is sex for Paul?

Sexual sin turns up regularly in Paul's vice lists. Three times he says 'those who do such things shall not inherit the kingdom of God' (1 Cor 6:9-10; Gal 5:19-21; Eph 5:5). He has quite a lot more references to sexual morality than the Gospels, including quite a lot of extra Greek terms. In the wider Graeco-Roman world, where sexual behaviour was more lax, Paul had quite a lot more to grapple with. A lot more could be said here.

2. What kind of sex really matters for Jesus and for Paul?

2. (a) key Greek terms in the New Testament for sexual sin

We come back to the key vocabulary of the Gospels. The Greek root *moich-* refers to adultery: trespassing on a marriage; it is a violation of the exclusivity of the marriage commitment. Prior to Jesus, adultery wronged a husband, and not a wife; Jesus insisted on parity.

The Greek root *porn* relates to any form of unsanctioned sexual intercourse; it is the Greek equivalent for the Hebrew *zanah* of the Old Testament. It is used of rape (eg. Gen 34:31), prostitution (eg. Deut 23:18 (ET v 17)), of sexual infidelity by one engaged to be married (eg. Gen 38:24), of adultery (eg. Jer 3:1-2), of incest (eg. Sir 23:17 (ET v 16); cf Lev 18:6-18), of sex between singles (included in Mt 15:19; 1 Cor 7:2) and would also apply to homosexual intercourse (cf Lev 18:22; 20:13), etc. Whereas the *moich-* word group focuses on the breach of relationship involved, the *porn-* word group focuses on the illicit erotic act as such.

2. (b) Sexual sin that mattered to Jesus

Well, clearly, we can start from adultery. The adultery words are more than twice as common as the *porn* words in the Gospels. While there is quite a lot of adultery around, it is not so common to speak in praise of adultery. However, Jesus spoke against not just physical adultery, but also adultery in our thought lives (Mt 5:27-30). Self-indulgent sexual imaginings are already a violation of the exclusivity of the marriage commitment, a breaking of faith with one's spouse.

The standard translation equivalents for the *porn-* set of

words are 'fornicate' and 'fornication'. But the language of fornication tends to obscures a simple fact: in the Jewish context of Jesus' day, and in the Christian context that grew out of it, the *porn-* words automatically embraced, as we have seen, rape, prostitution, sex between singles, the various forms of incest, also sex with animals, and finally same-sex sexual engagement.

2. (c) Sexual sin that mattered to Paul

Adultery was just as problematic for Paul as it was for Jesus, and he makes regular use of the same *moich-* and *porn-* language. But working in the wider Graeco-Roman world Paul widened his vocabulary to make sure that his hearers would recognise that he was sweeping into his net all forms of sexual irregularity. He has terms to deal with the moral uncleanness of illicit sex, the licentiousness of illicit sex, terms for men having sex with men, different words for the different roles taken by gay sexual lovers, etc.

A similar sort of broad understanding of the *porn-* root is clear from the varied uses Paul makes of it. The *porneia* in 1 Cor 5:1 is a form of incest, but by the time we reach vv. 9-11 the scope has broadened and the *pornos* will be the one who is involved in any form of *porneia*. If we may judge from 1 Cor 6:15, the *porneia* that is mostly in view in v. 13 is use of prostitutes. The use of *porneia* in v 18 is still part of the same development of thought, but is likely to be generalising and therefore broader, which is likely to be the case for the next reference as well, in 7:2.

When we get to 2 Cor 12:21; Gal 5:19, *porneia* no longer stands alone. Paul lines up with it *akatharsia* and *aselgeia*. But with the extra terms he is helping to create a perspective on *porneia*, perhaps in part to signal the wider reach he intends for the term. *Akatharsia* is literally 'uncleanness'. *Aselgeia* is conduct that emerges from a lack of self-constraint. It is doing what comes naturally, when what comes naturally is inappropriate because it violates an important boundary.

Paul varies his terms. In 1 Thes 4:3-5 the alternative to *porneia* is either continence or marriage. 'Holiness and honour' expresses positively what *akatharsia* expresses negatively, while *en pathei epithumias* ('in the passion of desire') plays an equivalent role to *aselgeia*. And there is more along these lines.

However, Paul also introduces specific discussion of homosexual sex, which might in the wider world not always be recognised as covered by the *porn-* root. The first half of his list in 1 Cor 6:9-10 of things that exclude one from the kingdom is made up of sexual sins and idolatry. *Porn-* and *moich-*, but then we get as well *malakos* and *arsenokoites*. The meaning of the latter is clearer, since it echoes the language of Lev 20:13. It is the man who 'beds a male'. The former involves a euphemism: the word means literally 'a softy', but it probably forms a pair with the latter, distinguishing a passive and active partner in homosexual sex. Paul picks out homosexual sex again in Rom 1:26-27; this time he doesn't use special terms, but simply describes male sexual pairing and female sexual pairing.

3. Why is the Bible so concerned to strictly channel human erotic activity?

The Bible is not so invested in strictly channelling human erotic activity because Christians are just killjoys. It is about protecting something that is precious.

3. (a) There is no narrow focus on sex

In 1 Cor 5-6 Paul is focussed almost entirely on sexual matters, but it is really important to note that in framing his discussion he is very careful to set his challenge in the sexual area into a bigger context. He wants it to be recognised that sexual sin belongs with a whole range of other sins which are just as damning. His kingdom-excluding list in 1 Cor 6:9-10 includes thieves, the rapacious, drunkards, revilers, swindlers.

Paul's list is of serious wrongdoing. No kind of sin is unimportant, but Paul does not treat all sins as equal.

3. (b) But sexual sin has its own special problems

1 Cor 6:18 says 'Every sin that a person commits is outside the body; but the fornicator sins against his own body.' This is a striking statement about sexual sin. Paul has a similar statement in Rom 1:27.

For the first part Paul is likely to be echoing an idea we can trace back to Jesus (see Mk 7:15, 21-23). Sin is the active fruit 'out there' of what is 'in here'. Sin defiles precisely because it is a putting into action out there of an inner evil impulse. In Paul's language it operates outside the body.

But there is something more with sexual sin. Paul also wants to say sexual sin makes an impact as well *in here*, or as Paul puts, the person sins against their own body. There is a double whammy!

3. (c) Paul's argument

The part of Paul's argument for restricting sexual activity that interests us here can be put quite simply. To put it crudely, his use of 'the two will be one flesh' from Genesis implies that sex is for gluing two people together permanently into a single unit.

Paul makes appeal to Genesis. The creation patterns are really important for him. Just as Jesus does, Paul considers that the creation accounts provide fundamental insight into what it is to be human and into God's vision for human well-being. So Paul appeals here to Gen 2:24, 'the two will become one flesh'. He is appealing to a key element of a biblical understanding of sex.

Sex, Paul is asserting, makes its own vital contribution to the formation of the psychosomatic unity of husband and wife. A man and a woman well glued together is God's pattern for the main kind of fundamental human unit within society. There are lots of other bits to the gluing, but sex makes a distinctive contribution.

Well glued together, a husband and wife, with their combined resources, are in a position to address the range of issues that life will throw up for them. Sex bonds them into a unique form of partnership for life. Well glued together they can provide the stability that will serve the needs of the children likely to be born from their sexual union. Well glued together they constitute a focal unit in the context of their wider family links, their local community and wider life.

If sex is a vital glue for marriage, then sex outside of marriage is using the glue in the wrong place. We might be able to give a sophisticated description of this gluing role in terms of brain chemistry, hormones, emotional consequences and so on. But Paul settles for the Genesis language of 'one flesh', which he sometimes paraphrases as 'one body'.

Compared to other modes of human intimacy, sexual intimacy creates a distinctive kind of openness between a man and a woman, which is at the same time a boundary marker between the couple and others.

Other kinds of sex create confusion about this most important boundary and create relationships that seem to have an inherent instability in them.

It is well documented that women who were sexually abused as children tend to have difficulties with sexual boundaries. They have these difficulties not at all because they want to be open to fresh abuse, but because the normal built-in instinctive mechanisms have been damaged by that early abuse. It is almost like something of a colour-blindness in this area. Even people who cohabit before marriage have more difficulty maintaining the boundaries to which they have committed themselves in marriage. And even more so, those who have had multiple partners beforehand have rather less likelihood of staying glued in marriage. If we are to believe the statistics that emerge, gay monogamous relationships are characteristically not exclusive, and are only rarely life-long. It is likely that one of the factors involved here is the misuse of the gluing process involved in their relationships. In these relationships there is only a pseudo-gluing or, to put it less tendentiously, an inferior gluing.

Conclusion

I set out to show that sexual morality really matters both to Jesus and to Paul. I have explored something of the range of sexual misconduct covered in Biblical sex ethics. And I have tried to clarify why it is that sexual misconduct matters so much. Sex has a bonding function, a gluing function. The misuse of this function defies God's creation pattern and messes up the proper function of sex.

By God's grace there is a recovery path from every kind of sin and from every kind of disaster. To our brokenness it is God's desire to speak mercy. But to our attempts to act in defiance of his standards God must speak to us in harsher tones.

11

EQUIPPING YOUNG PEOPLE:
SEX-PROOFING YOUR TEENS

Dr Lisa S. Nolland

I have spent decades working with teenagers and their families in various capacities. I believe that many parents have little notion of how important their role is, nor, given the pressing challenges young people face in 2017, what is at stake.

It hurts to see the disconnection and dysfunctionality which dominate the relationships of many adolescents and their parents. Because sexual matters are perceived as veritable minefields, this article will deal specifically with how to empower parents to up their game in this sphere.

Though I address parents – well-meaning, hard-working but often confused and struggling mothers and fathers – I preach to myself here as well (I am both a mum and step-mother). Though we all want the very best for our offspring, who does not find parenting a challenge?

Through teens' eyes: 'If you could read my mind'

Many teens feel fairly alone in life, except for their mates upon whom they depend. They speak one language while we answer in another, and inhabit yet a third in terms of ideas, values, technology, expectations, etc. Because adolescence is naturally a time when youngsters ought to be gaining more independence, it is hard to get the balance right.

Bickering and rows keep erupting but often teens do not

know what actually happened or why. They experience us as busy, stressed, worried and/or inaccessible. They know they are loved but find negotiating life together a minefield.

Through parents' eyes: 'Toto, we're not in Kansas anymore'

Many of us are simply too tired, busy or invested elsewhere. We feel (hope?) our youngsters are fine and need less from us now that they are 'grown up' (ish).

Indeed, many fail to fathom how treacherous and toxic youth culture can be. We keep referencing chapters from our past experience. Thus, though some aspects remain the same, others are fundamentally and profoundly different, but the truth of the latter may have passed us by.

When the reality hits of how different life is for many teens, parents can be tempted to give up, fearful they will just make things worse.

Sex-proofing teens: necessary but not for the faint of heart

First, sex-proofing teenagers involves discovering what they are presently being taught or groomed to accept as 'normal' in school and/or other youth groups. Many do not even know what the curriculum is, or seem aware that curricula vary hugely depending upon the presenter and school.

Because we understandably want to think the best of the Christian Head or that lovely youth worker, we tend not to check the accuracy of the 'advice' they give our teens on 'safe' sex, condom effectiveness, STIs, risks of increased partners and types of sex; body physiology, etc. See Note 1 below for more resources; I run seminars on this topic which is vast in itself.

We need to affirm the good while challenging the bad. At the time of writing, we can still exercise our right to remove secondary school youngsters from SRE (Sex Relationship Education). Do this if you think it necessary. Groups like C4M, Support4theFamily, Family Education Trust, Christian Concern and Christian Institute monitor these developments, so sign up for email updates from at least some of these groups so you can be fully informed.

Regardless of external input, teens need to hear our views, experiences, etc. Indeed, we should have been talking to our youngsters about sex, bodies and morality from early on, and modelling positive, biblical values in our daily lives. If this has not happened, then it is not too late to start. The Medical Institute for Sexual Health's *Questions Kids Ask about Sex: Honest Answers for Every Age* (2007) is a great resource.[2]

One further comment here. Many of us carry scars from our sexual pasts, abortions, etc., which ensure we keep quiet when we should be doing the reverse. Perhaps you do not want to give a blow-by-blow account of your sexual history, but your youngsters need to know that you have personally discovered that sex is fire (see below), and you want to spare them what you endured. If you need help coming to terms with a troubling past – understanding what happened, repenting, giving and receiving forgiveness, and letting God heal those memories – get help to do so.

Your kids need you to be fully present and engaged as they negotiate far more dangerous waters than we ever faced during our adolescence.

Sex messages

We must ensure our young people know we want the best for them! That is why we want them to push 'pause' on sex, because for adolescents sex can be toxic. It may look enticing but can take a huge toll, in the long and often short run. In particular, we want our teens to understand these sex messages:

Sex is fabulous. Sex is fire. Sex is for love and marriage. There is always forgiveness and a fresh start. Learn from past mistakes to become a wiser, stronger person better able to help others in similar situations.

Indeed, sex for them now is sad and stupid. We want them to be 'sex smart'! Sex is like smoking but much worse. One cigarette is not a game-changer, whereas one sex act gone wrong can be. It is that potentially serious and life-altering. Contra much modern SRE, sex is a big deal.

Smart kids are now understanding the deleterious impact of smoking on their health. I believe that model is a good one in this sphere as well. For the very religious, the fear of the Lord may give them the wherewithal to flee temptation, but many others need something more tangible and immediate. Harnessing the need for self-preservation can serve that end.

Framing these messages

Below are several ideas for facilitating your relationship so you can give the necessary input. And for older teens, and even young adults, it is never too late! Though some modification may be needed, you are and always will be their mother or father. The parental bond will never stop being vital.

Firstly, see your role as their mother or father as your most important job in life, ever! If you have made mistakes and not asked forgiveness, do so. They know your imperfections only too well. If there is something of a stalemate between you two, ask them to forgive you and then give your relationship a new start. Tell them you want to be a better mum or dad and need their help to do so. This does not mean going soft on boundaries, consequences or moral issues, but it does mean prioritising this relationship.

You were there when they were born and you will be there when they land their first job, walk down the aisle or have their first baby. What other adult has that privilege and responsibility? You see the bigger picture in a way they cannot at this stage of life.

Secondly, fill their 'love cup' each day with the four As: Affirmation; Attention; Affection (emotional and physical); Advocacy. Some adults fear their youngsters will become 'proud' or 'full of themselves', and so fail to give positive input. In my opinion this is totally wrong. Young people desperately need healthy affirmation from their parents. In relation to the final A (Advocacy), they need to know there is nothing they will ever do which will make you disown them; you will discipline them (or whatever) but you will always be their mother or father and be there for them.

Thirdly, become intimately acquainted with your teen and their world. Get inside their heads and learn to see life through their eyes. They will love it that you understand them and how they tick so well and you will handle messy, ambiguous situations far more wisely and effectively.

Under this rubric, learn to ask open questions: 'How do you feel about...?'; 'Why did you say that...?' Also, learn to ask them to tell you what they believe you said. What you said is often quite different from what they thought they heard you say, so checking it out is vital. With some, eye contact is difficult so lowering the intensity by doing something else while talking can be helpful.

As Dr Meg Meeker notes, 'Don't treat your son like the bad kid— no son will listen to a parent who assumes the worst of him. Remember, you're not the enemy (our toxic media culture is). Make sure he knows that.'[3]

Fourthly, facilitate the development of a solid psycho-sexual identity in your teen. The temptation to experiment sexually lessens if there is a healthy core identity. It spares teens at least some of the dabbling around trying to discover 'the real me'.

Fifthly, help them to understand their temptation cycles and how to break them. Do they recognise what pushes their buttons and why? Help them develop the necessary strategies and create the resources which will enable them to break the cycles and respond in healthy ways. As Simone Weil once noted, 'All sins are attempts to fill voids'. What voids are they trying to fill in sinful ways, and what healthy replacements can be made?

Sixthly, see yourself as your teen's coach or mentor. You do not live their life for them and have no desire to be a helicopter mum or dad. However, you have wisdom which comes from tracking their development over the years and also you are an adult with a developed pre-frontal cortex (where executive function/judgement occurs). This gives you an automatic advantage over your teen.

Encourage exploration of life goals, projects and investments in others. What are their aspirations and how are they going about fulfilling them? How are they helping others? Insist that they contribute to the family. Last time you checked there was no Maid Service, and Mum (or Dad) are not there to cater to their whims. Kids/leisure/entitlement/money/consumerism is a lethal combination and feeds a demanding self-absorption, immaturity and unhappiness.

Finally, chose your battles! What can you put up with? Not everything is equally important. Start to pray regularly with someone about issues which arise, and for your youngsters' present and future.

Notes

[1] For example, see Dr Miriam Grossman's excellent: http://familyfirst. org.nz/wp-content/uploads/2013/06/Miriam-Grossman-R18-Report-Executive-Summary-4-page.pdf which gives a brief range of concerns of much present SRE. It omits teen neuropsychology and the dangers of anal intercourse and early sexual debut. It downplays the negative impact of certain STIs or an STI diagnosis and overstates condom effectiveness.

It omits the vulnerability of the immature cervix etc. For more see: http://www.miriamgrossmanmd.com/learn/; also https://www.mercatornet.com/conjugality/view/robbing-children-of-their-innocence/18012 which has a great deal on adolescents (not just children) and 'comprehensive sex education', which some of our SRE actually is. Finally, see also Gabriele Kuby, *The Global Sexual Revolution* (English ed; 2015), pp 216-232.

For more on parenting of teens, see http://www.acpeds.org/parents/sexuality/sexual-responsibility-2/suggestions-for-parents-and-teens and http://www.huffingtonpost.com/dr-meg-meeker/sex-why-we-hate-talking-a_b_148810.html

[2] https://www.amazon.com/Questions-Kids-Ask-about-Sex/dp/0800732170

[3] http://www.huffingtonpost.com/dr-meg-meeker/sex-why-we-hate-talking-a_b_148810.html

All sites accessed 10th November 2016.

12

KINSEY

Dr Lisa S. Nolland

In this chapter I focus on something which I believe is vital in understanding the pan sexual assault on our children. This is the notion of children as sexual beings.

Who is responsible for this messaging? I would like to move our discussion now to Dr Alfred Kinsey (d 1956) of the University of Illinois, and Father of the Sexual Revolution. It is he who insisted that children were sexual beings from the womb, and indeed were legitimately deemed to be both sexual subjects and objects.

Alfred C. Kinsey

Kinsey was an entomologist who collected and classified eight+ million wasps. He was not a student of human biology or psychology.

Rather, Kinsey had a vested interest in promoting a radical pan sexuality. As a sadomasochist, he would insert objects like pencils and toothbrushes up his penis and suspend himself in the air by a rope tied round his scrotum. He struggled with impotence.

Kinsey's 'academic' team filmed themselves having different kinds of sex as part of their 'research'. During intermission his wife would refresh the actors and actresses with milk, cookies and towels!

Kinsey had hundreds+ of male partners. His marriage and family life were shams. He died an early death from self-inflicted sexual wounds.[1]

Kinsey's research

Kinsey was a sex addict whose PR spin (aka 'research') duped a gullible public. Looking back over the decades, it is plain to see that 'liberating' sex a la Kinsey has actually ended up in massive increases in STIs, illegitimacy, abortion, rape and divorce. His ideology was developed to justify and promote his perverse sexuality under the guise of 'science', 'health' and 'freedom'.[2]

Kinsey
Examples of Multiple Orgasm In Preadolescent Males

(Male Report, Table 34. P. 180; abbreviated)

Age	No. of Orgasms	Time Involved
5 months	3	?
11 months	10	1 hour
11 months	14	38 mins
2 years	7	9 mins
2 years	11	65 mins
2.5 years	4	2 mins
4 years	6	5 mins
4 years	17	10 hours
4 years	26	24 hours
7 years	7	3 hours
8 years	8	2 hours
9 years	7	68 mins
10 years	9	52 mins
10 years	14	24 hours
11 years	11	1 hour
11 years	19	1 hour
12 years	7	3 hours
12 years	3	3 mins

I do not believe his 'research' on child sexuality has been replicated elsewhere. See for instance the Table 34, from his seminal work, *Sexual Behaviour in the Human Male* (1948).[3] Indeed, it would be unethical to replicate measuring the number of 'orgasms' in babies and boys with a stop watch! Note how one youngster had a 10-hour, two others a 24-hour session of abuse at the hands (literally) of a Kinsey 'researcher'. These 'orgasms' were evidenced by such phenomena as fainting, screaming, having convulsions and fighting to get away from 'the partner' (as well as allegedly wanting more).

Men who 'love' children

Adult advocates of 'boy-love' such as NAMBLA (North American Man/Boy Love Association) have been delighted by Kinsey's research.

According to *The Age Taboo* (1981), 'Gay liberationists in general, and boy lovers in particular, should know Kinsey's work and hold it dear... Implicit in Kinsey is the struggle we fight today'.[4]

NAMBLA is keen to promote intergenerational relationships, or, as its website notes: 'It's the love of a man for a boy, and of a boy for a man. Enjoyable, consensual, beautiful.'[5]

Half-way stops

Not all would want to go the distance, as it were. Some would only go half way. 'Loving' children, i.e. finding oneself with a paedophile 'orientation', is seen as legitimate as long as there is no sex involved. Virtuous Pedophiles and B4U-ACT are two of the leading groups promoting rights for this sexuality. They cannot help having these feelings, it is claimed, and thus are victims par excellence.

Boys who are themselves 'boy lovers'

Things get even more difficult, however. Groups like B4U-ACT claim that lads become aware of their 'orientation' to paedophilia while still young. Even worse, they claim these lads are damaged by 'stigma'.[6]

Where we are at now

In the UK, youngsters are increasingly regarded as sexual beings, thus tacitly educated to 'develop their sexuality' as well taught about adult sexuality.

The Age of Consent in the UK is technically and legally 16. However, in practice it is slipping to 13, and even younger, according to anecdotal evidence I am hearing.

One popular UK example of sexual 'health' is Brook's 'traffic light tool'. It lists green, amber and red sexual behaviours that educators should look out for among children and young people.

For 13- to 17-year-olds, normal behaviour includes interest in pornography, sexually explicit conversations, and consenting to oral or penetrative sex (vaginal and/or anal) with someone of the same or opposite gender.[7]

As the Age of Consent is lowered, and as youngsters are seen as sexual agents, intergenerational sexual relationships become a real possibility. Kinsey would be proud!

Kinsey stands alone

According to educational historian Mary Shivanandan PhD, not one of the following theorists advocated sex for children, let alone adult sex acts with children. She had in mind: psychoanalytic theorists Freud and Erikson; maturational theorists Gesell and Havighurst; cognitive theorists Piaget, Kohlberg and Bandura; humanists Rogers and Maslow; and even B F Skinner.[8]

Conclusion

In order to counter this madness, we need to start taking the gloves off this ideological movement which is targeting our children and young people. We need to expose the real Kinsey and his actual views, demand accountability from leaders who promote them and expose the damage they have done. Enough is enough! Groups like Mass Resistance are doing just that, and are a great start in showing the rest of us how it can be done.[9]

Notes

[1] Judith Reisman, PhD, *Sexual Sabotage: How one mad scientist unleashed a plague of corruption and contagion on America* (2010) and http://www.drjudithreisman.com/. Miriam Grossman MD, *You're teaching my child what?* (2009), pp 20-34 and http://www.miriamgrossmanmd.com/a-brief-history-of-sex-ed-how-we-reached-todays-madness-part-ii/. James H Jones' *Alfred C. Kinsey* (1997) is deemed the authoritative biography of Kinsey, and Reisman and Grossman quote from it extensively.

[2] http://www.drjudithreisman.com/archives/2014/02/comprehensive_s_1.html; https://passthetorchblog.wordpress.com/2015/09/23/sex-and-children-the-toxic-impact-of-the-sex-ed-industry/ Reisman's video on bottom.

[3] http://www.drjudithreisman.com/archives/2010/10/table_34.html; http://www.drjudithreisman.com/archives/2016/11/wnd_exclusive_l_1.html

[4] http://www.drjudithreisman.com/archives/2007/06/namblas_website.html

[5] http://nambla.org/whatis.html

[6] http://www.b4uact.org/know-the-facts/faq/

[7] https://www.brook.org.uk/our-work/the-sexual-behaviours-traffic-light-tool

[8] Reisman, *Sexual Sabotage*, p. 174

[9] http://www.massresistance.org/

All sites accessed 10th November 2016.

13

THE MYTHOLOGY OF THE LGBT LOBBY
THROUGH THE LENS OF A LITERARY CRITIC

Julia Gasper

This book is called 'The New Normal'. I think that the attitude we should take is to remain very sceptical when people tell us that the abnormal is normal.

In our lifetimes, the LGBT movement has carried out a coup-d'état in the Western world. Armed with huge funding, it has taken over political parties, governments, education systems, and the media, to impose its agenda on most of the population. But history tells us not to despair when an extremist or aberrant agenda takes over. In ancient Rome under the Emperor Heliogabalus is said to have participated in human sacrifice; but when he was deposed this ceased. During the French Revolution, a new calendar and clock were imposed with ten months in the year and only ten hours in the day. The result was chaos. Then the law was repealed by Napoleon. In Communist China and Russia, in the twentieth century, private business was banned; in both countries today it flourishes again. In the USA in the 1920s, alcohol was banned, but those Prohibition laws were rescinded. So stay optimistic! Laws come in; laws go out.

The way we should be confronting the LGBT movement should be by pointing out its complete lack of any foundation of evidence either in the sciences or the humanities. The LGBT movement is not like the Black Civil Rights movement in America. That had solid evidence on its side, from science and the humanities. Science exposed the superficiality of difference between darker and lighter-skinned human beings. Literature, music and history demonstrated the intelligence of black people. In the case of homosexuality, there is no evidence for it being (as is claimed) innate, nor for it being normal, healthy, safe, or a viable alternative for a society to pursue collectively if it wishes to survive. To ask for tolerance is one thing, to impose a dogma of equivalence is quite another.

The writings of prominent homosexual icons themselves contradict the dogmas that the self-appointed leaders of the LGBT movement are imposing on society. Prominent among them is the 'born that way' myth. If the 'born that way' theory were true, we would expect the writings of homosexuals to bear it out, but instead we find the opposite.

Let us begin with Oscar Wilde, perhaps the most famous 'gay icon' and one who is quite wrongly held up as a martyr. Wilde's novel *The Picture of Dorian Gray* is now regarded as a classic of homosexual fiction. It is now set as a text for school study and fairly pedestrian 'notes' about it appear online. Written at a time when explicit reference to any sexual behaviour in a novel was taboo, the book skirts around the subject of homosexuality with innuendo and euphemism. It presents seduction as non-physical and substitutes sleazy opium dens for the male brothels that Wilde haunted with his sexual predator chums. We have to read the sub-text.

Wilde's novel certainly does not confirm that anyone is 'born gay'. At the outset, the young Dorian is definitely heterosexual, and early in the book he falls in love with a young actress named Sybil Vane and wants to marry her. Then he is led astray by two older homosexual friends. One of them is the artist Basil Hallwood, who paints the portrait of Dorian and becomes somewhat infatuated with him. Dorian, we are told, is a 'young Adonis, who looks as if he was made out of ivory and rose-leaves'. Basil compares him to Antinous, the young man beloved of the Emperor Hadrian (he died in mysterious circumstances, theories ranging from suicide or voluntary human sacrifice to murder). Basil introduces Dorian to another friend of his, the upper-class Lord Henry Wootton, a cynic and sensualist who lolls around smoking opium-tinged cigarettes, and says that 'conscience and cowardice are the same thing'.

Lord Henry is an obvious homosexual, who proclaims that the world needs to forsake mediaevalism and return to what he calls the old 'Hellenic ideals'. There would have been plenty of people in Wilde's London who knew this meant homosexuality. There was a very active pro-homosexual movement in Victorian England that used the cultural prestige of ancient Greece to give respectability to coarsely physical acts with rent boys. They wrote books and articles and ran their own magazines. Lord Henry proclaims, 'The mutilation of the savage has its tragic survival in the self-denial that mars our lives ... the only way to get rid of a temptation is to yield to it'. He flatters Dorian, telling him that he is marvellously beautiful, and youth and beauty are the only things worth having. He also disparages women, saying they 'have nothing to say and they say it charmingly'. Gradually, Dorian comes under Lord Henry's spell.

The languid and affected Lord Henry is actually married and quips that marriage 'makes a life of deception absolutely necessary for both parties'. It certainly made a life of deception necessary for Wilde himself, who was married with two children. Wilde was heterosexual until seduced by his younger friend Robert Ross, who then introduced him to the homosexual network in London. The novel hints at the guilt he felt about betraying his own wife. Lord Henry says many very negative things about women, in gibes and put-downs, which we are meant to regard as witty. 'She set out to found a salon and only succeeded in opening a restaurant.' And so does the narrator, constantly repeating that women's voices are shrill and their conversation boring. 'There are only five women in London worth talking to,' says Lord Henry. And he smiles about women being obsessed with looking young: 'As long as a woman can look ten years younger than her own daughter, she is perfectly satisfied.' This is odd as he and the narrator have already admitted a homosexual obsession with looking young. All this reveals a problematical aspect of homosexuality, that it entails an estrangement from the opposite sex, leading to an unhealthy division in society. It can be a form of apartheid.

What we do not find is any notion of people being predestined to be homosexual. The pivotal point of the story comes when Dorian makes the mistake of taking his two homosexual friends to the theatre to watch Sybil Vane act. Until this time, his passion for Sybil is intense. When he kisses her, he feels a thrill of extraordinary passion. He says, 'I love Sybil Vane, I want to place her on a pedestal of gold.' He proclaims, 'She is divine beyond all living things.' But when he returns, accompanied by the two older homosexuals, they have a marked influence on him. It is as if he absorbs their temperament, their feelings and their standards of judgement. Lord Henry's condescending disdain for women and Basil's indifference are contagious.

Under their influence, he perceives Sybil differently. Her charm has vanished and her beauty seems less alluring. Every movement she makes seems false and even her voice no longer seems expressive or sincere. Dorian becomes disorientated sexually. Sybil is no longer attractive to him. In fact, he starts to find her pathetic and disgusting.

Since Wilde cannot portray a physical seduction, Dorian is seduced by Lord Henry's fascinating, witty talk, through all of which runs a rather prominent sub-text about homosexuality and rejection of Victorian values. Among those values are romantic love, marriage, and fidelity. Dorian goes to see Sybil and tells her he is very disappointed in her. He breaks off their engagement, cruelly, and she commits suicide. He feels guilty and for a long time has to escape revenge by her family. After that, he embarks on a life of scandalous debauchery, and we are told that there are all sorts of terrible rumours about him and what he gets up to.

The novel makes it plain that Dorian becomes homosexual because of Lord Henry's intervention in his life. The influence of an older man and implied seduction change him, affecting his emotions, his desires and his perceptions. He is twisted and the result of this corruption is Sybil's tragic death and his own descent into increasingly sordid vices. Lord Henry fades from his life, but other homosexual acquaintances take his place.

The episode in which Dorian blackmails his old friend Alan Campbell to dispose of the dead body of Basil Hallward, whom Dorian has just murdered, is enigmatic because it cannot be explicit. Campbell refuses until Dorian scribbles a threat on a piece of paper, a threat we are not allowed to read. Faced with it, Campbell caves in and agrees to commit the horrible deed. So, Wilde foretells his own disgrace and downfall, a downfall that was, by the way, fully deserved as he was a pederast who hired rent boys from the lower classes in London and on the Continent . He once said 'Little boys should be obscene and not heard.'[1] Saying that some gay men are paedophiles is now regarded as 'homophobia' – unless it is said by someone who has no moral objection to it. It is not the facts of Wilde's sexual activities that are in dispute, it is the morality of them that is now banned and criminalised.

So, we can call Oscar Wilde as a witness to prove that people are not 'born gay'. Evidence from surveys establishes that men are more likely to identify as homosexual if their first experience of sex was with another man, and this is on average at a far younger age than heterosexuals. Many are seduced and 'turned' while only 13 or younger. You can hear homosexuals on TV talking blithely about how they want to 'turn' people homosexual, although LGBT activists want to ban any help for those who want to 'turn' back the other way. This is ideological incoherence. We should take more notice of this kind of evidence from homosexuals themselves than of the dogmas of the LGBT movement.

The lesbian writer Radclyffe Hall agrees that nobody is born gay. In her classic novel *The Well of Loneliness*, a work of literary distinction written in the 1920s, she describes with candour the factors in environment that mould and determine a woman to become lesbian. Sir Philip and Lady Gordon are the owners of a fine estate, Morton Hall, in the South of England, and they want a son who will inherit it and carry on their name. They are happily married, yet ten years pass before they manage to conceive a child. Before its birth, Sir Philip has already chosen the name Stephen and talks about sending him to Harrow School, which is exclusively for boys. His wife Anna shares his conviction and during pregnancy imagines herself soon playing with a little boy. When the baby is born and turns out to be a girl, they still call her Stephen. Not surprisingly, she grows up somewhat confused in her gender identity.

Lady Gordon has no other children and so the father remains fixated on 'Stephen' as the nearest thing to a son he will ever get. Anna feels deep disappointment and never loves the child. Stephen is left in the care of a strict and unappealing nanny. At the age of seven, Stephen suddenly forms an attachment to a buxom housemaid named Collins. There could not be a clearer case of maternal deprivation. Stephen identifies with the male heroes in her storybooks and history books, because these are the sort of people her father wanted her to be. She identifies with Nelson, or even at times with Jesus. Brought up alone, with no siblings and no schoolmates, she has nobody to laugh her out of her misguided aspirations and delusions.

When she asks her father whether it is possible for her to become a man, Sir Philip does not give her any clear answer. He laughs and says that one day she will want pretty frocks. If he had said plainly, 'No, you can't be a man, but you could be a fine woman, it doesn't have to be about pretty frocks', the outcome might have been rather different. He knows that she is well aware of his desire for a son, and he never once apologises to her, or says that now he has a daughter he has changed his mind. He never grows any more positive about the daughter he has got. There are plenty of people whose preconceptions about the sex of their child are forgotten after birth; the child develops into a unique person and captures their affection. Not Sir Philip. He remains fixed and this damages his daughter more and more with every passing year. When he wants to pay her a compliment, her father tells her he is going to treat her like a boy. He buys her prints of Nelson, instead of Boadicea who might have been a more positive choice. He never tells her that girls can be brave too. Her mother also continues to daydream about the son she always wanted.

Stephen spends more time with her father than her mother. He teaches her to ride and fence. When she learns to ride it is astride, not side-saddle which was still the norm for women – or at least for ladies – in the Victorian era. Her father indulges her in this. They are both living in a fantasy world. Stephen never leaves this fantasy world. Her adult behaviour as a lesbian is an extension of it. When she encounters boys, she notices that they have a strong sense of privilege and superiority and this makes her envy them even more.

Stephen's case is rather comparable to that of Vita Sackville-West. Born to the last generation of the family that had owned Knowle, the great Elizabethan mansion, for generations, she was an only child but could not inherit the estate or the title because they were entailed. They could only pass in the male line. No wonder then that she had some sense of frustration, of inadequacy, and entertained fantasies of what it would have been like to have been born a boy. Surely this had some influence on her bisexual behaviour.

As Stephen grows up, her appearance does not help her to adopt a female identity. She is unusually tall for a girl and her figure is mannish. She has broad shoulders and narrow hips, and she is stronger than most women. She resembles her father so much that shopkeepers who knew him thirty years earlier recognise her by the likeness. A sense of being different from the current ideal of female beauty reinforces her reluctance to play the role. Stephen finds herself the object of unflattering remarks about her unfeminine height and flat chest and she is affected by this social pressure. Instead of telling people to shut up, she daydreams about becoming a man.

At the age of eighteen, she forms a strong attachment to a young man called Martin Hallam who returns her affection. Her parents encourage it, hoping that it will lead to love and marriage. Stephen likes Martin a lot as a friend but when he proposes to her she reacts with shock and treats him as if he has insulted her. It is a crisis. She has to confront the confusion of her gender identity and admit the truth or continue with her fantasy. She prefers to continue with the fantasy. By now, she is addicted to it. He hastily flees back to Canada, and she never gets another chance to marry. From that time onwards, she falls in love with women.

Compare the recent, tragic case of Nancy Verhelst, who died in 2013 at the age of 44. Dr Michael Brown has researched the background of this case and it makes tears come to your eyes. Born a woman in Belgium, Nancy wanted to be a man. She had a series of so-called sex-change operations and changed her name to Nathan at the age of 42. But she was never happy with the outcome. After the final operation she was still not happy. In fact, she was getting more and more miserable. Instead of realising her fantasies of virility, the operations just made her feel 'like a monster'. She had allowed doctors to injure and mutilate her, cutting off her breasts and sewing up her vagina, then attaching some tissue to her labia to make it look like a penis. She could never father a child, and never change her skeletal structure, but she could take artificial male hormones to encourage some beard and muscle growth.

Nancy/Nathan was so dissatisfied that she demanded the doctors end her life by euthanasia. Denying her own female identity had become such an overriding obsession that it was more important than life itself. Disgracefully, under Belgian law, a doctor could legally consent. A doctor carried out a lethal injection on the grounds that she was too depressed to want to live. Nancy's mother had always wanted a son. She made this preference abundantly clear and indeed took it to a psychotic level. Her mother rejected her from birth, having this to say after she received news of her daughter's death: 'When I first saw "Nancy", my dream was shattered. She was so ugly. I had a ghost birth. Her death does not bother me.' Such cruelty and callousness did profound damage. She continues, 'For me, this chapter closed. I'm not concerned about her death. I feel no sorrow, no doubt or remorse. We never had a bond which could therefore not be broken.' So Nancy/Nathan struggled with this pain of rejection from the time she was born right up to the time of her death: 'Hours before his (*sic*) death Mr. Verhelst had spoken of how, as a child, he 'was the girl that nobody wanted', describing how his mother had complained that she had wished he had been born a boy.

Radclyffe Hall's heroine suffers a similar deep rejection. In *The Well of Loneliness*, Lady Gordon goes on calling her daughter 'Stephen' even while condemning her, hurtfully, for being lesbian.

The Well of Loneliness[2] is a very valuable testimony and it needs to be listened to. There are many other respects in which it is politically 'incorrect'. For instance, when Stephen starts to mix in homosexual and cross-dressing circles, she notices that not everybody remains in this life. 'Pat's Arabella had suddenly married, having wearied of Grigg as of her predecessor. Rumour had it that she was now blatantly happy at the thought of shortly becoming a mother.' This prepares us for the novel's conclusion. Stephen's lover, Mary, becomes attracted to a man (none other than Martin Hallam), and he is in love with her. Stephen does a far, far better thing by feigning infidelity in order to send Mary into the arms of Martin. It is tragic and moving. It is also inconsistent with the idea that people are born homosexual and can never change or move on.

In her preface to the Virago edition, Allison Hennigan refers to Stephen as a person who is 'born with a male soul in a female body'. This quaint notion derives from the theories of Karl Heinrich Ulrichs, the German nineteenth-century author of *Forschungen Uber Dars Ratsel Der Mannmannlichen Liebe* (Researches into the Riddle of Love Between Men). He posited that it was possible for a male or female soul to somehow get born in the opposite sex's body. There are two things wrong with this theory. One is that most people today in the twenty-first century do not believe in a soul; the other is that if there is such a thing as the soul, it cannot have a sex because sex is physical. The soul by definition is not. Despite its illogicality, Ulrichs' theory has been revived in modern times by transgender theorists, who assert that it is possible to be 'born in the wrong body'. When you hear this theory, repeated by journalists and forced on children in our schools, remember that a way to refute it is to point out that it is not new, it is just a tired old theory from the nineteenth century that has been dug up and launched again from the grave like a zombie.

The third writer I will consider is the modern novelist Jeanette Winterson, a much-lauded writer, darling of the LGBT movement and the left-wing. Unlike many best-selling writers, Winterson has a literary flair. She can tell a story, can be poetic and also has a streak of black humour. Intentionally or not, her books confirm that nobody is born gay, and that the homosexual condition is a highly unsatisfactory one.

In her first book, *Oranges Are Not the Only Fruit*, Winterson is probably describing her own childhood. Whether or not we regard the narrator as identical with the author, the fact remains that her novel describes how a certain family environment leads to a certain psychological outcome, and this psychological outcome corresponds closely to Winterson's own case. Central to the childhood of the central character is her relationship with her adoptive mother. Married but childless, the mother preferred to adopt rather than to conceive a baby by marital love. Sex, even with her husband, was so repugnant to her that she would rather take a child from an orphanage than have connubial relations. For some reason, her husband does not divorce her although he would be perfectly entitled to do so. In their household, the mother and father have only a cold, distant relationship. The mother's real passion is for religion. She is a fanatical Pentecostal Evangelist and brings up the little girl to be a puppet for her fundamentalist beliefs. Controlling, obsessive, she shows some signs of paranoia, when she hoards food in a cupboard in case of another outbreak of war. She has peculiar ambitions for the girl and trains her to preach in public at an age when other children would be out climbing trees or playing with hula-hoops and skipping ropes. The protagonist is locked into a relationship with a mother whose alienation from the father means that she relies on the daughter for close affection. The daughter gradually becomes aware that preaching is not regarded as normal for females in this culture. So, while she does it precociously well, it also causes her a crisis of gender identity. She reads Jane Eyre and finds from that and many other sources that vicars have nearly always been men. Not surprisingly, she suffers growing insecurity and discomfort. In her late teens, she abruptly forms a relationship with a girl, and decides that her identity will be as a lesbian. She has not discovered something that was innate, rather she has continued down the path on which she was set by her upbringing. She has no model of a normal male-female relationship in her own family and has been deprived of nourishment for any heterosexual development. She has always been locked in a female-female relationship and she has gradually come to internalise her mother's horror of men and sexuality. To put it bluntly, her abnormal upbringing has led to her emotional and sexual preferences .

Throughout Winterson's novels, we find that an attitude to men and to sex that is one of disgust. Heterosexuality is portrayed as repellent and men are regarded as inferior to women. In *The Passion*, Napoleon Bonaparte is presented as an absurd figure, abnormally short (which is a myth – he was 5ft 7inches, taller than the average Frenchman of his time) and vain so that he insists on surrounding himself with short servants. His passion for Josephine is belittled: 'He liked her the way he liked chicken'. To men, women are just a piece of meat, nothing more. Men are frequently compared to animals, often to dogs: 'He was like a dog, he could close his eyes and sleep in a moment'. The touch of a man is perceived as an injury. When Napoleon touches the narrator's ear, he pinches it so that it was 'swollen for days'. When the narrator loses her virginity, she does so to a stranger who 'liked his women face down, arms outstretched like the crucified Christ'. There is no love and no healthy lust either. Sex is presented as an ordeal, almost a death, and men as killers. One of the central characters in the book is a fat, drunken ship's cook, a coarse brute despised by the narrator and lacking in any human characteristics. His desire for women is presented as disgusting. On a visit to a brothel, even the prostitute finds him repulsive and he treats her roughly and abusively. It may be that, to Winterson's mind, he represents all the physicality and animality that her adoptive mother found disgusting, and that she replicates her mother's neurotic attitude. His status as a hate-figure is reinforced when he reappears in the guise of the husband of Villanelle, the narrator's beloved. Now he is the object of jealousy as well as contempt. He has grown even more fat and coarse physically. He is a stereotype of unalleviated grossness.[3]

In *Written on the Body*, the female protagonist recalls losing her virginity to a man called Frank, who has the 'body of a bull' and wears gold hoops through his nipples. Unfortunately, he cannot resist joining them with a chunky chain and so the effect 'resembled a Chanel handbag'.[4] He represents repellent animality, and he is made to look ridiculous. Frank does not believe in love but wants promiscuity and the life of a sailor. Taking the phrase 'a wife in every port', Winterson tells us he wants 'a hole in every port'. To him, women are nothing more than an orifice. He is a sub-human brute, incapable of love, and walks out on her as soon as sex is over.

In *Lighthousekeeping*, we have another orphan protagonist, Silver, adopted by an old man, Pew, who is acceptable as he is like a grandfather to her, not in the same category as sexual men. The cold, prim schoolteacher Miss Pinch is reminiscent of the mother in *Oranges*. The second story told in the book, about Josiah Dark, displays all the hatred of men and sex so typical of Winterson's novels. Dark is a twisted sadist who beats his wife and verbally abuses her. He has no reason to hate her, but he bullies her and makes her horse bolt just to terrify her, and takes her out in a small boat in storms just to make her seasick. Winterson's description of their physical union is disgusting. 'He turned her face down, one hand against her neck, the other bringing himself stiff, then knocked himself into her in one swift move, like a wooden peg into the tap-hole of a barrel. His fingermarks were on her neck when he had finished. He never kissed her.... When he had finished with her, he sat across her, keeping her there, the way he would keep his dog down when he went out shooting. In the chilly bedroom, he let his semen go cold on her before he let her get up.'[5] We are told that he once loved a girl but did not marry her. Winterson describes men who behave like brutes, sub-human, and despicable. Later the book features a lesbian love scene which is rather banal, and perhaps too obviously autobiographical to be interesting as fiction.

Men, as portrayed by Winterson in her books, are just beasts. Their love is only sexual appetite, and that sexual appetite is something women ought to fear because it consumes and degrades them.

This pervasive negative attitude to man-woman relationships may appear offensive to heterosexuals in the context of an LGBT movement that reviles them for expressing even mild reservations about homosexuality.

In *Art and Lies*,[6] Winterson describes how a beautiful Spanish girl comes to work in England. Her employers make her sleep in the attic and very soon the husband rapes her. 'My father in gabardine saw her body in its summer dress, and tore it until she was naked in the bleaching air.' (No explanation of why the air bleaches.) 'Naked under his panting clothes' (a metonymy, presumably, as it wasn't his pants that were panting), 'naked under the caustic of his skin, naked he had her and naked he drove her away.' In Winterson's work, the embrace of a man is always evil and dangerous, even to another male. In the same book a male protagonist, Handel, describes how he was loved in his youth by a homosexual Roman Catholic Cardinal. He returns the Cardinal's affection, though understanding well that it is homosexual, and spends an idyllic summer with him in Venice. They sleep in the same bed, and the Cardinal arranges for the boy to be castrated before he returns home. When his parents discover it, they decide not to make a fuss.[7] One wonders if there would have been an outcry by the LGBT lobby if a heterosexual writer had written something like this, portraying a paedophile castrating a boy, and reducing him to a eunuch as well as a catamite. Perhaps because it was written by a lesbian, it passes with approval.

To sum up, while Wilde, Hall and Winterson may be very talented writers, and they are held up as iconic by the LGBT movement, their books do not confirm the assertions of that movement. Instead of saying that they are born homosexual, they offer honest and valuable testimony about some of the environmental factors, from birth onwards, that can affect people's future sexuality and gender identity. And they provide evidence that people who have for one reason or another become homosexual are not in an optimum state of well-being. No single writer's work can be taken as a single, final and sole explanation of every sort of homosexual behaviour, but it pays to take a critical stance about the canon of 'gay' literature and re-read it in a way that deconstructs

LGBT arguments. If the writings of homosexuals themselves contradict the dogmas of the movement, we should use them to reveal the confusion of that movement, in which may lie the seeds of its own demise.

Notes

[1] See McKenna, Neil, *Secret Life of Oscar Wilde* (Century Books 2003)

[2] *The Well of Loneliness* (Virago), 357.

[3] *The Passion*, 36, 18, 70, 15.

[4] *Written on the Body* (Penguin), 93.

[5] Winterson, *Lighthousekeeping* (Harper), 54-55.

[6] Winterson, *Art and Lies* (Vintage Books), 205.

[7] *Art and Lies* 196-201.

ABOUT THE CONTRIBUTORS

Carlos D. Flores studied philosophy at University of California, Santa Barbara, where he graduated with honours. He has written on matters of philosophy for various publications and his works have been translated into various languages.

Julia Gasper is an academic who has taught at various universities and written books on English literature and history. She is the author of *Elizabeth Craven, Writer, Feminist and European* (2017); *The Modern Philosopher, Letters to Her Son and Verses on the Siege of Gibraltar, by Elizabeth Craven* (2017); *The Marquis d'Argens, A Philosophical Life* (2014); *Theodore von Neuhoff, King of Corsica, The Man Behind the Legend* (2012); and *The Dragon and the Dove, The Plays of Thomas Dekker* (1990).

Brittany Klein holds a Master of Fine Arts degree from the University of Virginia and teaches college English. She is co-author of *Jephthah's Children* (2016) and serves as a Council member of the International Children's Rights Institute.

James D. Lopez was born and raised in Los Angeles. He graduated *summa cum laude* from Indiana University where he majored in political science and is now pursuing graduate studies. He is a student fellow at the Love & Fidelity Network and a Youth Council Member at the International Children's Rights Institute. His writings have appeared in The Federalist, Public Discourse, The Stream, Indiana Student Daily, and he has blogged at: www.ThemBeforeUs.com.

Robert Oscar Lopez is author of *Colorful Conservative: American Conversations with the Ancients from Wheatley to Whitman* (2011), *Jephthah's Children* (2016), and *Wackos Thugs & Perverts: Clintonian Decadence in Academia* (2017). He has taught at universities since 1999, including at California State University where he was a professor from 2013. In 2016 he resigned on the grounds that he could not uphold his Christian faith in a secular teaching position. He currently teaches at Southwestern Baptist Theological Seminary's L.R. Scarborough College as a humanities professor.

Daniel Moody is a philosopher specialising in the relationships between bodies, minds, words and laws, and is the author of three books exploring the origins and implications of the notion of self-chosen legal identities: *The Flesh Made Word: A New Reason to Be Against Abortion* (April 2016), *The Flesh Made Word* (Expanded Edition; August 2016), and *The Flesh Made Word: No Ordinary Lie* (November 2017). He blogs at gentlemind.blogspot.co.uk, and can be followed on Twitter @DanielMoodyFMW.

Carys Moseley works as policy researcher for Christian Concern, as well as for the Presbyterian Church of Wales. She studied Classics and Theology at Cambridge, Oxford and Edinburgh Universities, and has taught Theology, Christian Ethics and Latin at Edinburgh University, Sarum College and Swansea University.

John Nolland, PhD (Cambridge), is a professor and long-standing faculty member of Trinity College Bristol, where he has at various times been Head of Biblical Studies, Course Leader, Academic Dean, Vice-Principal and Acting Principal. He has written technical commentaries on

Luke (Word Biblical Commentaries) and Matthew (New International Greek Testament Commentaries). He has published in many scholarly journals and written chapters for many academic books. He has been a Visiting Professor at the University of Bristol.

Lisa Severine Nolland, MA, MCS, PhD (Bristol) is Convenor of the Marriage, Sex and Culture Group of Anglican Mainstream, Oxford. Her academic work includes *A Victorian Feminist Christian: Josephine Butler, the Prostitutes and God* (2004) and 'Josephine Butler and the Historian: Critic and Friend' in *Sex, Gender and Religion: Josephine Butler Revisited*, eds. J Daggers and D Neal (2006). She also edited and made major contributions to *God, Gays and the Church: Human Sexuality in Christian Thinking*, eds. L Nolland, C Sugden and S Finch (2008).

Peter Saunders originally trained as a General Surgeon but since 1992 he has served full-time with the Christian Medical Fellowship, a UK-based organisation with 4,500 UK doctors and 1,000 medical students as members, first as Head of Student Ministries and since 1999 as Chief Executive.

Rick Thomas was formerly a GP and later worked part-time in hospital respiratory medicine whilst also involved in church planting and leadership. He has an MA in Bioethics and Medical Law from St Mary's University (London), and is a researcher with the Christian Medical Fellowship.